the happiness trail

About the book

We live in a fast-paced and highly competitive world. The last few years have seen changes not witnessed in centuries. Have all these developments increased our sense of well-being? Data seems to suggest otherwise!

The Happiness Trail shows us an attainable, contextual way to achieve two seemingly complimentary goals, happiness and success, that we many a time discover to be contradictory.

In this book Ramesh Venkateswaran lays down five easy-to-follow approaches to a happy and successful life, which he calls the five I's: Integrity, Interact, Involve, Imbibe and Impact. Armed with this road map, the ever-elusive happiness seems within reach and success a natural consequence.

Praise for *The Happiness Trail*

Just as classical history dwells on the past, older (and wiser) folks tend to live in the archives of their experiences. History that is lively enough to guide future minds is vastly different both in content and energy. Here is a book by an older and wiser professional that achieves the same—it is energetic, philosophical and incisive. Ramesh Venkateswaran is particularly well-positioned to have attempted this—and he has surely succeeded.

R. Gopalakrishnan, former Director, Tata Sons, and Vice Chairman, Hindustan Unilever

There is a not a lot of wisdom in the world today, but we can find it in this book, as it explores everything from individual integrity to corporate fraud. It is a guide to making decisions that can lead to a happy, meaningful life as well as a better society. The examples and messages are timeless.

Michael A. Cusumano, Deputy Dean and SMR Distinguished Professor of Management, MIT Sloan School of Management

The Happiness Trail is a must-read that explores the true meaning of happiness in a refreshingly down-to-earth and novel fashion, with nuggets of wisdom in each chapter that are bound to motivate readers to introspect and develop personalized plans to lead happier lives. Beautifully crafted in a conversational, non-preachy style and peppered with apt anecdotes, crisp examples and succinct pointers, the book is a page-turner and a pleasure to read.

A. 'Parsu' Parasuraman, Emeritus Professor of Marketing and James W. McLamore Chair Emeritus, University of Miami

Ramesh Venkateswaran writes with a simplicity which is refreshing and a candour which is incisive. His clear message, that success does not equate to happiness, has been reinforced multiple times. The issues of stress, mental health and hectic lifestyles aimed at achieving goals have been tackled with a keen understanding from years of experience as coach and mentor and an alternate way of thinking about these issues has been articulated with clarity.

It is an extremely relevant book in these frantic times and will benefit a wide cross section of readers from youth who are beginning their professional journeys to seniors who are about to conclude theirs.

Geet Sethi, Padma Shri, former World Billiards Champion

Given his rich accomplishments in fields as varied as engineering, management, education and mental health, Ramesh Venkateswaran is eminently qualified to bring focus on the challenges that await our Gen Z and millennials as they emerge into a highly competitive world. Defining the fine line between success and happiness, he points out the moral dilemmas and practical pitfalls that lie ahead. This book provides, across age barriers, a pragmatic road map for life that is signposted for sensitivity and compassion unto others and ethical conduct for oneself.

Admiral Arun Prakash, former Chief of the Naval Staff

Eminently readable and brilliantly insightful. Ramesh Venkateswaran helps you make the distinction between the desire for success and the quest for happiness through examples drawn from sound family values, his stint as a corporate professional and later as a leader in academia. These are interspersed with his readings from, and interpretation of, classical philosophy and psychology, before he signs off with the five I methodology he has developed to bring lasting happiness to the reader.

M.M. Murugappan, former Executive Chairman,
The Murugappa Group

In the mad quest for name, fame and money, we often lose sight of what really matters. In this insightful book, one of our most thoughtful alumni fills this gap by providing an easy-to-follow GPS to happiness. Essential reading in these troubled times.

Rishikesha T. Krishnan, Director,
Indian Institute of Management—Bangalore

Through his book *The Happiness Trail*, Ramesh has succinctly outlined a legacy of practical wisdom for the younger generation, but it has something for everyone. His rich experience in the field of academics across prestigious institutions comes alive as he shares his reflections and insights on life—from parental dilemmas to never-ending pressures—and makes the reader question assumptions on concepts like success and happiness and their interplay. Ramesh's ability to connect the dots across different sectors and generations makes for a fascinating read.

Hema Ravichander, Strategic Advisor and Independent Director, Marico Industries and Indian Hotels Company Ltd

It is said that knowledge tempered with judgement is wisdom. I have known Ramesh for several years and have benefited greatly from his knowledge and experience. He has compiled years of his life's learnings to develop an amazing road map for the youth, in particular. *The Happiness Trail* is a terrific read and helpful for everyone.

Venky Mysore, Managing Director, Kolkata Knight Riders, and CEO, Red Chillies Entertainment

Happiness is a virtue worth pursuing. It is what makes the world a better place and drives human relationship. Ramesh's book shows a way to achieve genuine happiness.

Arun Balakrishnan, former Chairman and Managing Director, Hindustan Petroleum Corporation Limited

The Happiness Trail is extremely readable and spiced with several examples and experiences that help bring clarity to the reader. Ramesh has brought much practicality to a fuzzy subject such as happiness. And to me the best part of the book is the toolkit of five I's that it provides in conclusion. It would appeal to the young and old, parent and child, as well as student and teacher.

Bhaskar Bhat, Director, Tata Sons, and Chairman, Vistara Airlines

the happiness trail

A ROAD MAP TO SUCCESS

RAMESH VENKATESWARAN

HarperCollins *Publishers* India

First published India by HarperCollins
HarperCollins *Publishers* in 2021
An imprint of HarperCollins Publishers
HarperCollins *Publishers* India, Cyber City, Building 10-A, Gurugram, Haryana-122002, India
www.harpercollins.co.in

2 4 6 8 10 9 7 5 3 1

P-ISBN: 9789354892103
E-ISBN: 9789354892189

Typeset in 11.5/15.7 Adobe Garamond at
Manipal Digital Systems, Manipal

Printed and bound at
Manipal Technologies Limited, Manipal

*

HarperCollins *Publishers*, Macken House, 39/40 Mayor Street Upper, Dublin 1, D01 C9W8, Ireland

This book is dedicated to my parents
Lakshmi and S.S. Venkateswaran
Who taught me by example

This book is for
Karam, Ria, Anirudh and the Alpha generation
May you find happiness

Contents

Part 3

Foreword

IN THIS EXTREMELY COMPETITIVE WORLD of abundant opportunities, small family sizes and parents willing to give their children anything, happiness has become a highly complex and, to a large extent, an elusive goal for many. The young adult is ambitious, demanding and often laidback. She has a huge canvas of opportunities and yet is often confused. This has resulted in general higher levels of stress and poorer mental health. The last eighteen months of the pandemic have only accentuated the problem. Despite substantial improvements in the quality of material life, happiness is something many of us are always searching. In our pursuit of success we often miss out on happiness.

At a time like this, *The Happiness Trail: A Road Map to Success* is most fortunate. This book covers with a spark of genuineness, simplicity and clarity on how to pursue two seemingly complimentary goals, happiness and success, that we many a time discover to be contradictory.

Ramesh and I have been friends for over three decades. My connection with Ramesh, however, goes back to about fifty years ago where he was my senior at IIT Bombay. I have been amazed at how he threw out the security and the lure of the corporate world to find more meaning to 'living' in its true sense. He has donned many hats—corporate executive, independent management consultant, high school head, B-school director, mentor for many, active involvement in social projects, chairperson and volunteer at an NGO co-founded by him and a long-time faculty at the prestigious IIM Bangalore. Each time I would wonder how he landed there and what he would do. Every time he stepped out of his comfort zone, he has done so with energy and enthusiasm. I have seen that each new role has been one of self-learning, personal growth and an inspiration for those he interacted with, especially a large number of young minds—from school children to college graduates. I know that Ramesh's father was an officer in the Indian Navy and also one of the first Indians to umpire at Wimbledon. I guess reinventing careers must be in his genes!

This book carries all these experiences and learnings, tried and tested by him and others over time.

I know that the insights he has shared are borne out of his first-hand interactions and track record of developing and building people across different age groups and in diverse settings. This book not only explores key issues of happiness and success but more importantly deals with the challenges in achieving happiness. It presents a compass to navigate through the anxiety and dilemmas that we face in making choices, as also a road map to translate intent into action and achieve happiness.

Though Ramesh's thinking comes from his personal experiences, I firmly believe that these are guidelines that anyone can use for getting personal happiness, irrespective of how we define success.

There is not a shadow of doubt in my mind that his interactions, experience and insights across the spectrum of his professional life hold him in good stead to write about success and happiness.

I am delighted to see the coming together of the book *The Happiness Trail: A Road Map to Success.* Now it won't be just those of us who have had the good fortune of knowing Ramesh that can benefit from his teachings but anyone and everyone.

I encourage you to embark on this promising journey and wish you a huge treasure of happiness.

Nandan Nilekani

Chairman and Co-founder, Infosys,
and Founding Chairman, UIDAI

Preface

HOW THIS BOOK HAPPENED?

THE IDEA OF THIS BOOK came in an email from an old classmate of mine. The message was that we were all getting on in years and that it would be a good idea to leave behind something substantial for future generations. She suggested that we could list out five things for our grandchildren that would help them lead happy, successful and meaningful lives.

Initially, I did not give the email much thought—it was one of those numerous messages one tends to get these days on various media groups that one is part of. As time went by, however, it struck me that in the preceding few years I had in fact been engaged in this topic, albeit not in the exact manner as articulated by my classmate in her email. But the email became the trigger for this book. Interestingly, she would not even know that she had sowed the seeds for this book since I never spoke to her about her email.

How exactly did this book come about? Let me explain.

After many years in the corporate world and as a private consultant and trainer, my career path took a huge turn. Without any planning or strategy, and purely by accident, I found myself in a fascinating world of young people. I was asked to head The Lawrence School, Lovedale, a heritage co-educational residential public school in Ooty (now Udhagamandalam) in south India. It is a 163-year-old school, located in the beautiful environment of the Nilgiri hills. The fact that the school was my alma mater only made the opportunity that much more exciting, my motivation to work there much more than it might have been otherwise, and the experience emotionally enriching and satisfying. After a short stint at The Lawrence School, I was extremely fortunate to head a graduate school of management—the Sri Dharmasthala Manjunatheswara Institute of Management Development (SDMIMD) in Mysore (Mysuru)—for four years. Thus, in a short period of six years, I got the opportunity to meet and interact with young people in the age groups between nine and twenty-five years from very close quarters and in fully residential environments. This gave me round-the-clock access to a completely different world—a world I had left behind many years earlier.

I have been extremely fortunate and privileged to have interacted with the younger generation and to have seen their world across multiple perspectives and conditions, and in a far more intimate and intense manner than would have been possible in a normal day school or college. In addition to this, I have been an adjunct faculty for over twenty-five years at a leading B-school in India—the Indian Institute of Management Bangalore. In this process, I have had the good fortune of meeting, teaching and getting to know some of the brightest minds in the country.

Adding to the series of chance events, I got into the field of mental health and counselling in 1991. I am a co-founder and volunteer at Vishwas, Society for Mental Health. Vishwas is a not-for-profit organization that offers free services to help people under emotional stress. All services are provided by trained volunteers on a completely pro bono basis. My work with Vishwas over the last thirty years as a volunteer, trainer and administrator has allowed me to see many facets of people from all walks of life which would not normally be evident to most others, even those close to them. This gave me a degree of sensitivity towards people that I am sure I would not have got otherwise.

As I reflected on my association and interactions with students and educational institutions and my work with Vishwas, I realized that in the last twelve to fifteen years as the head of these institutions, as an adjunct faculty and as a counsellor, I had actually spent a lot of time with students and older people discussing topics like happiness, success, values, principles, objectives of life, conflicts and dilemmas. It came to me that in all my interactions in these institutions and as an invited speaker at various events, there were common threads in what I was trying to convey. Interestingly, I would spend (and continue to spend) the final lecture of my courses on strategy at the IIM on matters related to the topics I have mentioned just earlier. This session in my programmes has been consistently well received by my students. Many would come and chat with me, based on this lecture. My lectures and these after-class sessions with many students became the triggers that helped me build on the original idea given to me by my classmate Vasantha in her email. The final lecture then took the structure of my 'five things to do for a happy, meaningful and successful life', which has been developed into the theme of this book.

Many of my former students will recognize a lot of what I say in the following pages. I hope you will get some insights and food for thought, as I have over the years, thinking about some very simple and basic aspects of our journey in life.

Ramesh Venkateswaran
Bengaluru, September 2021

1

INTRODUCTION: WHY THIS BOOK?

We are living in a fast-moving and highly competitive world. The last few years, or rather decade, have seen changes not seen in centuries earlier. Technology has been moving at an exponential rate, new products and services have changed the way we live, and physical and material comforts have never been better. Our physical comforts have increased multiple times in the last fifty years or so. Science, technology and medicine have certainly helped increase our life spans. No generation has had the kind of choice that we have today in just about any sphere of life. All these improvements and advancements should make current generations much better off than their parents and grandparents. Have all these developments increased our sense of well-being? We should, logically, be happier than earlier generations who had much less than what we have. But data seems to say otherwise and the jury would be out on this point. Interestingly, despite all the technological progress that was intended to make our lives simpler, our lives seem to have become more complex.

What is happening to us? Why is it happening to us? What is the impact of these changes on mankind today? What are the implications for future generations of mankind? And what can we do about it? These are issues that we need to understand and address as individuals who play various roles as we progress in life. These are questions which, in addition to ask of ourselves, are of great concern to parents who have to bring up children in environments that are very different from the ones they grew up in.

I am sure parents anywhere in the world want the best for their children. If we step into the world of a parent in India, it is quite interesting. There is a huge imbalance in the demand-and-supply situation when it comes to education and employment opportunities. Parents are worried about their children from the time of their admission in kindergarten and through their stint in school and into college. The worry does not seem to stop even after the children graduate from college. This makes it a good twenty-two years at a minimum, from the time a child is born till the time the child graduates, before Indian parents can heave a sigh of relief in terms of responsibility for their child's future. This is, of course, not counting the years for the child's post-graduate studies and then the years it may take for the child to get a good job.

I have taken the Indian scenario as the basis for discussing this situation since I am familiar with it and have seen it through various lenses. As I think about it, however, it is not very different in other parts of the world. From the day we are born we seem to enter a never-ending race to perform and achieve. The first part of this race is run by the parents on behalf of the children. They then supposedly hand over the baton to their children. But in India many parents never seem to hand over the baton fully. They keep running the race along with their children. As the children get older, they are often confused and left wondering as to who is really running the race—them or their parents!

In their continuous anxiety to get the best opportunities for their children at various stages of their growing up, parents experience high levels of anxiety. This anxiety naturally gets transferred to their children, who are often on journeys not necessarily of their own making but those decided by the parents. This transfer of anxiety manifests itself as stress, and its resultant outcomes can be physical, emotional or behavioural in nature. In this process of continuously running a race to 'get ahead', many of us move on in life and find ourselves arriving at a destination, only to wonder what we are doing there and whether this was really what we wanted in the first place. The question we need to ask is, why we do what we do at each stage of our lives—from trying desperately to get into good schools, reputed colleges, striving for good grades, getting prized jobs in good organizations to moving up the ladder in the corporate world or in our chosen field or career. At the end of the day, what are we looking for from each of our actions?

At a basic level, I think what we want ultimately is to be happy. But what we are in fact chasing is success. In some implied manner, we believe that if we are successful in each of our actions and activities, we will get what we want and thus we will be happy. If I work hard in school and get good grades, I will get into a good college. I go to coaching classes and tutorial institutions so that I can get into good colleges of national/international repute. If I get into a good college, I will get a good job in a good organization. If I get into a good organization I will get paid well. I will have a good reputation and status, which will be the path to even better jobs in the future. When I get paid well, I can afford a lot of the material comforts.

Thus, success at each stage will get me personal satisfaction, money, status, material comforts, reputation and recognition. When I have all of this, I will achieve my final goal—*I will be happy*. This example can be extended to any chosen career path for most of us—whether it is art, music, research, writing, teaching and so on.

We believe that if we are successful, by whatever yardstick we define success, we will be happy.

In a manner, we believe

SUCCESS = HAPPINESS

This sounds simple and logical enough, and willy-nilly we get into a continuous race to chase success. Is it this easy in reality? Does this simplistic formula work? Unfortunately, it does not work out this way for many of us, as we will see in the pages that follow. We need to turn the question over.

I believe the way to look at it is: I am successful if I am happy.

HAPPINESS = SUCCESS

I submit that our goal should be to pursue HAPPINESS and not SUCCESS.

What This Book Is About: The Wisdom of Age

This book attempts to explore our quest for happiness and success and the challenges we face in achieving them.

An Amazon search for books on happiness books will fetch over 70,000 results. A search for books on success will also give you around the same number. Over the years, enough has been said and written about happiness and life. Books on these subjects have been authored by people from just about every field—from religion, spirituality, philosophy and sociology to the corporate world. I do not fall into any of the above-mentioned categories, so the book is not written from the perspective of any of them. This book is also not a self-help, do-it-yourself book with some quick fixes to get you to being happy and successful.

When it comes to philosophical subjects such as happiness, success, the meaning of life . . . one tends to use what I call the *wisdom of the ages* as a backdrop. The wisdom of the ages has come to us distilled over the years through religions and civilizations, through the scriptures, and from great philosophers and thinkers. In this book, however, I make no attempt to use religion or philosophy as a backdrop. As a person who has seen life through different lenses and has gone grey over the years, I have thought of existential issues at a very operational level. In the process, I believe I have gathered some wisdom and insights to share and leave behind for future generations. I am, therefore, resorting to what I call the *wisdom of age* as my message to my grandchildren and the younger generations.

Since the original trigger was to list five messages to convey this wisdom, I have restricted my points to exactly that many! The reader may well ask if these five points are adequate as a guide to achieving happiness and success. As in matters of personal life, there is no right way or only way to convey wisdom. When one listens to the words of wise men and women over the ages, one realizes that in essence they are not saying anything very different from one another. My five I's capture the core of the path to happiness. Yes, these five could well be seven or nine! In the following pages, I share my road map for a happy and meaningful life.

The 5 I's for a Happy and Meaningful Life

I believe my five I's are valid, irrespective of how one defines success.

Success is a subjective and personal matter. Success could be money in the bank, material possessions, designation, social impact, public visibility, recognition, personal sense of achievement, self-actualization, or whatever. There is certainly no absolute benchmark for happiness and success. I have, therefore, made no attempt to prescribe what success is or ought to be. What I hope this book will do is to serve as a guide to the final destination of happiness, irrespective of how one defines success. The challenge is to give a broad-spectrum prescription for a specific desired outcome.

The five I's is my road map to help navigate a life journey in this complex world where the desired destinations keep changing, as also the paths to getting to there. I make no claims to any research or originality in the pages that follow, for the simple reason that most paths on this subject by experts in the field are generally pointed to very basic and simple directions. I also understand that there will be more ways of looking at this subject and presenting a prescription. As the old Hindu saying goes:

> Truth is one. Paths are many.

When I reflect on my five I's, I am convinced that this is a good road map for most of us to use as a guide in our life journey. It is simple to understand and easy to execute. The five I's have been culled from my personal experiences and journey, from my discussions and interactions with many people far more wise and experienced than I am, from the teachings of the generations before mine, from the intuitive wisdom of young people, from the many after-class discussions I have had with my students and, most importantly, from common sense.

How to Use This Book?

I have structured this book into three parts:

Part 1: It is necessary for you to get a grip on this part so that you have a context to the main purpose of this book. We look at what it is that we are trying to achieve in our lives and what is happening around us that often makes it difficult to get what we want. In Chapter 2 we look at happiness and success—two elements that are at the centre of our lives in some implied manner. In Chapter 3 we look at the competitive world of today and the pressures it places on us to perform. In Chapter 4 we discuss the implications of these pressures and the consequences if we are not clear about and conscious of what can happen to us if we are not careful. This section will address three important questions—why it is important for you to take stock of where you are; what you are trying to achieve; and what is happening around us that are obstacles or roadblocks in our journey.

Part 2: In this part we discuss my GPS for happiness and success through the five I's. This part deals with the 'how to get what I want'. The five I's are the outcome of my experience and learnings. The chapters in this part can be read in any order.

Part 3: I end this book leaving you, the reader, with some thoughts on the issues you will face in getting to your goals of happiness and success. I hope you will see the relevance of the five I's in helping you navigate your life using them. I also give you a simple plan you can use to validate my five I's framework and calibrate it for your own journey.

Who Is This Book For?

This book is for *you,* irrespective of your age and background. Since you are reading this book, I take it that you are over twenty years of age. If you are a Gen Z (born after 1995) or Gen Y reader (born 1981–1995), then this book is meant to help you think through your life's journey. If you are a Gen X reader (born 1961–1981), this book will help you think through not only your own journey but will also give you some pointers and guidance for your discussions with your children. In the unlikely event that you are a baby boomer (born pre-1960), then in all probability you are my friend and are reading this out of your natural goodness and friendship with me! You will also probably be a grandparent. That would be ideal. That was the idea from which the book took off in the first place. This book is for your chats with your grandkids. There are no better people than grandparents when it comes to connecting with the younger generation.

I have written the book as a chat with a young adult. It should make for easy reading. I hope you will find the next few pages easy to digest and yet goad you into thinking and acting. This is so that when you reach a destination in life you are sure you wanted to get to you are not left wondering what you are doing there, as often happens with many of us. It will also hopefully get you to think of where you want to go in the first place and help you plan your journey.

Cheers—to happiness, meaning and success!

PART 1

2

HAPPINESS AND SUCCESS: NOT TWO SIDES OF THE SAME COIN

THINK ABOUT IT. We do not like to go to places that make us unhappy. We do not like to be with people who make us unhappy. We don't like to be unhappy. Period. On the other hand, we love to go to places that make us happy—restaurants, shops, events. We seek people who make us happy. We want to be happy. Throughout our lives we strive to achieve happiness.

The path to happiness, many of us believe, lies in achieving various milestones, goals and targets that we set for ourselves. Achieving these milestones is a measure of what we would call success. We then assume that by being successful we will achieve our goal of happiness. In short, as mentioned in the earlier chapter, we generally believe that success and happiness go together and that being successful will result in our being happy.

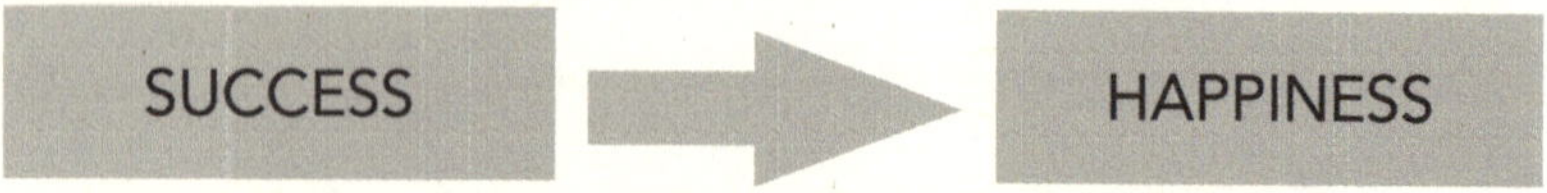

Unfortunately, this is more a myth than a reality, if not seen in the right perspective. Let's look at what can happen. What do the words 'success' and 'happiness' really mean? When we talk of happiness, do we truly understand what it means and, more importantly, what it implies? To understand this better, let us step back and take a closer look at success and happiness.

Success Is Never-Ending: Happiness Is Ever-Eluding

Success: Favourable or desired outcome

Going by the meaning above, success is defined as an outcome (result) that was desired (goal). Thus, when we reach a goal or milestone, there is an element of success. A student getting good grades, an admission into a good university, a great job, someone putting in a great music performance, creating an award-winning film, owning a dream car or house, winning a gold medal in a national or international event, winning a reality show, and so on, would all qualify as yardsticks of success for the people concerned. As we normally understand and expect, a person's achievement of his or her goal should result in the person being happy because one has got what one wanted.

Now, let us look at what happens when we get what we have wanted. Once a set goal is achieved, interestingly, that achievement is no longer relevant for future aspirations and goals. Fresh goals are set, and the journey continues.

Cut to real life. As a student appearing for a school-leaving exam, an immediate target (success) would be to score well in the exam as that will help the student get into a good college. The student gets good grades. Once the good grades have been obtained, the target now gets revised to getting into the desired college. In reality, of course, there is no guarantee that the student will get into the desired college if she gets good grades. The good grades are only a necessary but not sufficient condition for the admission. The student gets into a good college—success! The fact that the student is in the desired college is now no longer relevant. The goal is now to get good grades in college. Why? So that she will get a good job after graduation or entry into a good university for a post-graduate course. The student gets good grades in college. Success! Now the goal is reset—to one of getting a good job. The student gets a good job—in fact, the dream job that she wanted. Success! The next goal is to move up the ladder, which could be defined by many parameters—salary, title, bank balance, material possessions like car, house, club memberships. This process goes on and on and on. It is almost never-ending.

What is happening here? There is certainly a good feeling when one achieves one's goals and meets with success. There is a sense of joy or pleasure in achieving our goals. However, in each of the above situations, we see that this joy or pleasure is not permanent or long-lasting. In fact, in many cases I suspect that success will mean a sense of relief more than of joy! This sense of joy wears out soon enough because the goal has been achieved and is no longer relevant for the next part of your journey. Fresh goals will be set for the next part of the journey. We have added a new word—'pleasure'—which we will explore more of soon. Here is my realization:

> Success is not a destination but a continuous journey.

The definition of success keeps changing with the times and situations. In short, the goalpost keeps moving with each goal scored. There is no finish line when we can say that the race is finally over.

This brings us to the core of this book—by achieving success as defined above, would it result in happiness for the person? The hard truth is, not necessarily. Each achievement will most definitely bring in positive emotions. It can bring a sense of joy, pleasure, satisfaction or relief. But happiness? The contrary often happens. As we saw above, a target achieved is not generally relevant after the event. The effect of success wears out. Once the goal is achieved, there is now a need to set fresh goals. A person's new goals are often influenced by his or her earlier experience of success. They come with higher expectations and the pressure to continue to achieve more. This, of course, can spur a person to higher performance and achievements, or can result in disappointment and unhappiness, depending on the extent of pressure and the nature of the goals that have been set—more about this later. The cycle of continuous resetting of goals is almost never-ending, as shown in the figure below.

What do we really experience when we are successful? When we achieve success, we believe we are happy. We shall now see if it is truly happiness that we experience.

In addition to 'happiness', words like 'pleasure' and 'joy' also connote a feel-good, positive state of mind. These words are often used interchangeably with happiness. We will limit our discussion to just one of them—pleasure. This is not meant to be a book on psychology or philosophy. For this book, however, I will attempt to differentiate between happiness and pleasure. Can these two words be used interchangeably? Do they convey the same emotion? Let us look at whether they do, especially in the context of their relationship to success.

The Hedonic Treadmill

Happiness: A state of well-being and contentment
Pleasure: A state of gratification

Happiness, by the above definition, is a 'state' of contentment and a subjective sense of well-being. Pleasure, which is also subjective, is what we feel when something good happens to us. The description of the state is of gratification. It is essentially a feeling that is triggered by an external event—good grades, dream college, birth of child, winning of a lottery, purchase of one's first home . . . Positive experiences certainly make us feel good and give us a sense of what we loosely call 'happiness'. However, as we have seen earlier, this so-called positive state does not last permanently. Over time, we return to the status quo ante because our feeling good was dependent upon external events and experiences. We thus see that what we experience is really pleasure.

At the cost of repeating myself, for the purposes of this discussion we can say that pleasure is essentially the feeling we experience when we meet our goals, which are the triggers for our feelings of enjoyment, satisfaction, etc. These good feelings are short-lived, since we now have another set of goals and benchmark for success and our energies are directed towards achieving those goals. We believe that if we achieve a particular goal we desire, we will be happy. For example, I have always wanted to drive a particular car, or have pinned my dreams on a particular house, job, or whatever. When I get what I want, it will give me great pleasure, which I would understand as happiness.

What psychologists say is that the good feeling one gets upon achieving a goal tends to fade away over a period. The process by which positive or negative effects on happiness fade over time is called *hedonic adaptation*.[1] The concept says that people tend to have a base level of happiness called 'set point', and they repeatedly return to their baseline level of happiness, regardless of what happens—positive or negative—to them.

During the late 1990s, this concept was modified by British psychologist Michael Eysenck. A success triggers a burst of joy or pleasure and temporarily changes the status quo. This may result in people often adjusting their expectations to the new status quo and finding themselves desiring even more to maintain the same level of happiness. This cycle he called the hedonic treadmill.[2] We pursue pleasurable things because we think they'll make us happy. When we finally achieve or acquire what we're seeking, we adapt to our success in a short period of time and our success no longer gives us pleasure. As a result, we begin seeking something new, and the cycle repeats. Eysenck thus compared the pursuit of happiness to a person on a treadmill, who has to keep working just to stay in the same place. The thrill of the new car, dream house, title won or plum job shrinks with the passing of time.

The Hedonic Treadmill in Action

In layman's terms, what I understand is that hedonic adaptation essentially means that once one achieves a goal, the achieved goal effectively becomes the new normal. Hence, any satisfaction or dissatisfaction will be with reference to the new benchmark. I can see myself going through this process as I write this book in the middle of the Covid-19 pandemic. After being an envious 68kg to 70kg in weight for many years till my early thirties, I gradually climbed the scale to reach a steady 88kg, where I remained for the next twenty years or so, until recently. Initially, I used to long to get back to my 70kg days, until it finally dawned on me that this was a distinct impossibility. I reset my expectations to a realistic weight of 84kg. I believed that I would be really happy if I could hit this target. Interestingly, during the pandemic months of 2020, I not only hit this target, I actually came down to a weight of 80kg. Once my weight steadied at 80kg, two things happened. Firstly, if my weight went over 81kg it worried me. Secondly, I now long for a weight target of 75kg—80kg is now longer good enough! In a short span of seven months, a dream goal has become the new normal. Welcome to the hedonic treadmill.

We thus see that success in achieving a target or goal generally results in pleasure more than happiness. Before long, your new car, new house, new job and good grades will blend into your surroundings and your mind will fixate on something else to pursue in the quest for happiness. I am sure we would have all experienced this many times in our lives. To put it simply, pleasure is dependent on external triggers, while happiness is independent of them. To sum up, happiness is the feeling of being satisfied with life, feeling positive emotions, feeling enjoyment. This happiness is a state of inner fulfilment and stays over a long period of time. It is not momentary; it is a feeling of contentment and well-being. Pleasure, on the other hand, is triggered externally and tends to be ephemeral or short-lived.

Pleasure can contribute to happiness, and happiness can enhance or deepen feelings of pleasure, but the two can also be completely mutually exclusive

> Now sometimes people confuse happiness with pleasure. True happiness relates more to the mind and heart. Happiness that depends mainly on physical pleasure is unstable; one day it's there, the next day it may not be. – Dalai Lama

What does this have to do with us? If we understand and accept the concept of the hedonic treadmill, we should be focusing on activities that give us happiness, which is long-lasting, rather than limiting ourselves to activities that only give us pleasure, which is more ephemeral or transient. In short, we need to relook at the way we define success. Does being successful make us happy, or can we say that if we are happy then we are successful, since happiness is the ultimate goal? In my understanding, rephrasing our perspective will help us evaluate our priorities and channelize our efforts and energies to have a lasting impact.

Happiness is largely our ultimate goal. Happiness is a state of mind. Let us take a look at what could prevent us from reaching this elusive goal called happiness.

Happiness—A Mirage: Are We Really Happy?

Success is very personal. It is as defined by an individual for himself or herself. For one person, a measure of success is the bank balance; for another it is the readership of her blog; for a third could be the fact that he could cure a group of drug addicts or alcoholics; and for a fourth it may just be mastering a musical instrument. As the old saying goes: 'One man's meat is another man's poison.' There is no one way to describe or decide what success is. That is why we need to take a serious look at what success really means to each of us individually. In our life journey, we have a final goal of happiness, which we hope will be achieved by our meeting intermediary milestones or goals. Achieving these goals will be indicators of success. So, in some intuitive way, we all probably believe:

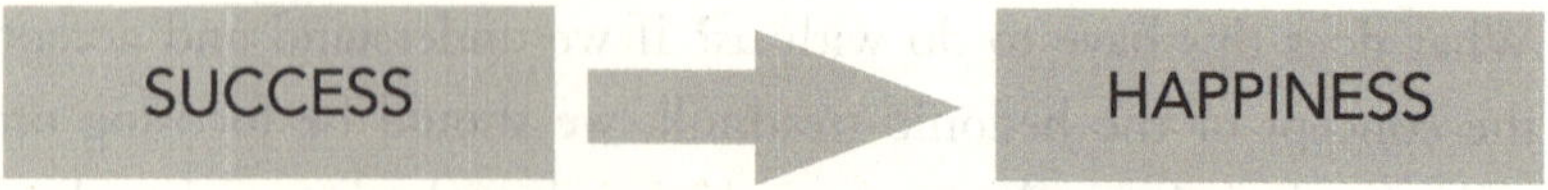

Σ Success=Happiness

For any journey we need to know what our desired destination is. Equally importantly, we need to know why we want to get to that destination. Are we really clear about our desired destination? To arrive at a desired destination and to plan our journey, we also need to know our current location—where we are now. This will initiate the process of assessing the factors that can facilitate or impede our efforts to reach our destination, and consequently might help us to relook at the paths we need to take to achieve our goal. Or even reset our goals. Since what one sees as success may not be seen in the same way by another, it is important for each one of us to first define what success means to us and then work out the details of our journey.

> If you don't know where you are going any road can take you there. – the Cheshire cat, *Alice in Wonderland*

We will now shift our attention to what is happening around the world in the context of improving one's wealth, material benefits and happiness. There are too many factors that that can make happiness elude us. We will see that happiness will not come about by chance.

Happiness—In Which Direction Are We Headed?

The world has indeed moved at an amazing speed in the last few years. Products and services that were part of science fiction just fifty years ago or less have become household realities in a short span of time. Video calling would have been unthinkable twenty years ago. Today it is available to just about every person anywhere the world. Video streaming, driverless cars, smartphones that pack in more power than a desktop computer did thirty years ago, artificial intelligence, big data . . . You name it, it was not around when your parents grew up. In fact, a lot of what you use today was probably not around even when you were in school! In terms of material and physical comforts and opportunities, it would be safe to say that all of us today are far better off than at any other time on this planet.

For all these developments, is the world a happier place to live in? Are we really better off than our predecessors, both physically and emotionally? Unfortunately data seems to point to the contrary.

Between 2010 and 2018, the US's per capita GDP went up from US $36,334 to US $54,541. This works out to a 50 per cent increase. Intuition and common sense would point to much higher levels of happiness and well-being in the country, with an average income growth of 5 per cent per year. Yet research suggests that American adults have been growing less happy since 2000. Adolescents have been experiencing more depression, suicidal ideation and self-harm since 2010. Negative feelings—worry, sadness and anger—have been rising around the world, up by 27 per cent from 2010 to 2018.[3]

The chart below, showing the average happiness and per capita GDP in the US for the period 1972–2016, says it all.[4]

Average Happiness and GDP Per Capita, 1972–2016

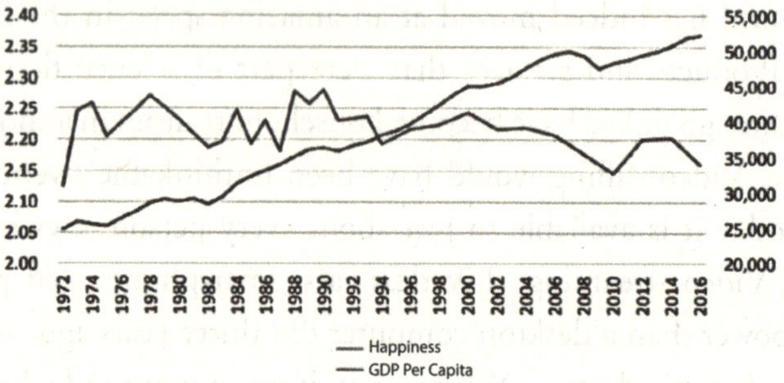

This continuing fall in the general levels of happiness in the world has its effect on all of us, both physically and emotionally. There is a link between mental health and happiness, so let us spend some time on this aspect of health. We will then address a much talked about and important malady that affects us all—stress—and its impact on happiness.

Mental Health and Happiness

Good health has two components—physical health and mental health. The adage 'healthy body and healthy mind' succinctly describes the role of the two.

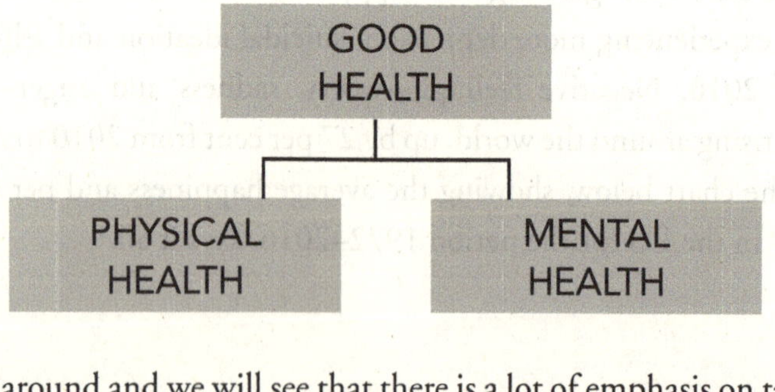

Look around and we will see that there is a lot of emphasis on taking care of our physical health. The physical health industry is huge.

Items from clothing and accessories to gyms, fitness equipment and, now, wearables and apps make up a multi-billion-dollar industry worldwide. People have no problems talking about their physical health and the efforts they make to ensure good physical health. In fact, people often talk about their physical activities with pride and flout the brands that are part of this industry. Good physical health is no doubt important. The efforts expended and money spent on ensuring good physical health are well placed.

Talk of mental health, however, and there is generally an awkward silence and shifting glances. No one likes to talk about mental health. Despite all the advancements and progress in literacy and awareness levels, there is still stigma attached to mental health and issues related to it. Mental health is linked with the terms like 'mad', 'off one's rocker', 'crazy', 'loony' and so on.

The hard reality is that a healthy body results from good physical and mental health. There is a correlation between physical health and mental health. There is also strong relationship between mental health and happiness! Happy people are healthier, they have better relationships, make friends more easily and find more success in life. According to the 'Origins of Happiness' report of London School of Economics' Centre for Economic Performance, eliminating mental health issues such as depression and anxiety would increase happiness by 20 per cent, whereas eliminating poverty would increase happiness by only 5 per cent. In other words, tackling mental health problems would be four times more effective at increasing happiness than reducing poverty.[5]

Stress

Stress is a commonly used term, especially in the context of happiness and well-being. There are many contexts in which the term stress is used. For the purpose of this book, we shall use 'stress' as relevant to mental and emotional well-being and happiness.

Stress: a physical, chemical, or emotional factor that causes bodily or mental tension and may be a factor in disease causation

This book is not expected to go into the technical aspects of psychology and stress. It is, however, useful to keep in mind some simple and basic concepts of stress as relevant to the purpose of this book and our normal day to day life. Generally, the term stress is used in the context of the negative impact of stress, as in 'she is very stressed at this moment' or 'he is on medication because of high stress'. Stress is really what happens to a person inside the body as a result of a trigger. There are three terms that need to be understood in the context of dealing with stress.

Stressor or stress factor – a stimulus or trigger that causes stress

Stress reaction – the response or impact of the stressor on the individual

Stress – what happens inside the body as a result of the stressor

In common parlance, when we say 'stress', we are generally referring to the stress reaction and not to stress as defined. For example, my friend was really stressed out before an interview. He was so worried that he couldn't sleep the whole night and was completely blank at the interview.

Stressor or stress factor	: interview
Stress reaction	: worry; sleeplessness; going blank in the interview
Stress	: the body's internal response to the stressor (interview) that resulted in the stress reaction (worry, sleeplessness, going blank)

Stress by itself is not a bad thing. We all actually need a certain amount of stress to keep us performing. There are thus two types of stress:

- There is good stress called *eustress*—a positive form of stress that has a beneficial effect on an individual. Eustress helps and spurs us to perform.
- There is bad stress called *distress*—a form of stress that works negatively on us physically, emotionally or behaviourally.

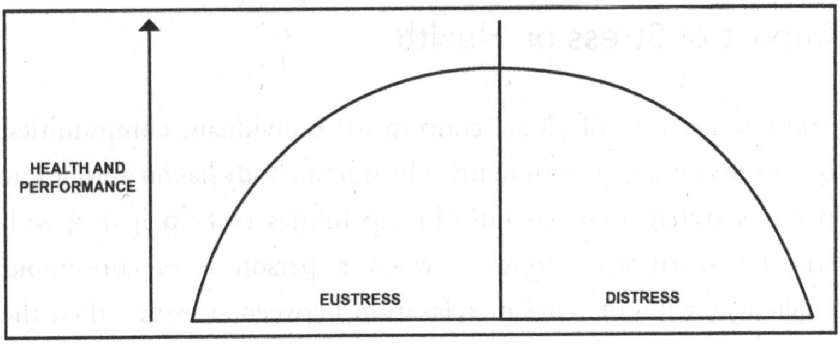

We all need a certain level of stress to perform. I am sure we have all heard of the 'butterflies in the stomach' phrase. A sense of nervousness, anxiety and uncertainty before some event. It is important to have this sensation or else one might get complacent or indifferent. I am sure even the greatest sportsmen and experienced speakers and seasoned professionals get butterflies in the stomach before an important event. The issue therefore is not about having stress but about managing it to ensure it works in our favour. What is important is to deal with this stress to spur you to perform.

The management of stress is nicely summed up in the following thought:

> It's OK to have butterflies in the stomach.
>
> The important thing is to make them fly in a formation.

Without getting further into a technical discussion on stress, we shall limit the discussion to something that affects the individual adversely (distress) and prevents a person from reaching his/her full potential. In effect, if there is physical or mental tension that affects a person adversely, it will be difficult for that person to be happy.

Impact of Stress on Health

Stress is a matter of global concern for individuals, communities, organizations and governments. The human body has an autonomic nervous system that has built-in capabilities to help it deal with stressful situations. However, when a person faces continuous challenges without relief or relaxation between stressors, then the effect of stress on this individual will be adverse. Prolonged exposure to stress factors and inability to deal with them take their toll on the person—both physically and emotionally. This can disturb the body's internal balance or equilibrium, leading to physical symptoms and emotional and behavioural problems.

The effects of stress and stress reactions manifest themselves in three ways.

EFFECT OF STRESS	SYMPTOMS
Physical	Headache, high blood pressure, chest pain, ulcers, diabetes, sleep disorder, sexual dysfunction . . .
Emotional	Depression, anxiety, low self-esteem, low self-confidence, fear . . .
Behavioural	Anger, withdrawal, relationship issues, chemical dependencies, like alcoholism, drug addiction . . .

Stress is linked to some of the leading causes of death, including heart disease, cancer, lung ailments and accidents.

Stress and Depression

One significant result of stress is depression. Depression is widespread and prevalent in large numbers of people. A major concern is the economic and social impact of depression. Every day people stay home from work, miss school, go to the doctor or even die because of the effects of stress. It is estimated that American employers spend US$300 billion every year on healthcare and lost workdays linked to stress. Up to 80 per cent of workplace accidents in the US come from stress or stress-related problems, like being too distracted or tired. Depression leads to US$51 billion in costs due to absenteeism and US$26 billion in treatment costs. Work-related stress causes 120,000 deaths and results in US$190 billion in healthcare costs yearly.[7]

More worrying is a 2017 study of over half a million eighth-to-twelfth-graders in the US, which found that the number of children exhibiting high levels of depressive symptoms increased by 33 per cent between 2010 and 2015. In the same period, the suicide rate for girls in that age group increased by 65 per cent.[8,9] A 2018 American College Health Association survey of more than 26,000 college students found that 40–60 per cent reported significant episodes of anxiety or depression during the year—an increase of about 10 per cent from the same survey conducted in 2013.[10]

The extent of the problem is further reflected in the sales of the pharma industry. The anti-depressant drugs market, valued at US$13.75 billion in 2016, is expected to reach $15.98 billion by 2025, with a compounded annual growth rate (CAGR) of 2.15 per cent over the forecast period. This number does not factor in the effect of the Covid-19 pandemic of 2020, which by any account has increased levels of anxiety, depression and other mental health-related problems. The improvements in GDP and standards of living do not seem to have had any significant positive effect on the reduction of stress.

As mentioned earlier, the effect of stress is multifold. The link between stress, medical problems and even death seems to be getting established. A major cause of concern is that currently the impact of stress is hitting people much earlier than it used to some years ago. Cardiologists at the Sri Jayadeva Institute of Cardiovascular Sciences and Research in Bengaluru, India's largest heart hospital, have been noticing a worrying trend: the number of heart-attack cases among thirty to forty-year-olds is on the rise. They studied about 2,000 such cases over two years. Factors such as diabetes, hypertension, obesity, physical inactivity or hyperactivity usually cause heart disease. Roughly 30 per cent of heart attack victims are from high-stress white-collar jobs.[11]

One final word about stress and its impact on us. Remember, when we say stress colloquially, we actually refer to the stress reaction. The stressor or trigger is not what causes stress. The individual's response to the stressor determines its effect on us. Here is an example I use as a starting point for our training on counselling and understanding people who are stressed.

Two students write an exam. Both get their results. Both students fail in the exam. One student dies by suicide and the other goes to watch a movie. The question is—was failing in the exam the problem? The answer is quite obvious—no. The problem is the response to the failure. The students reacted differently to the trigger of failure. The stressor is the same. The stress reactions were very different. Stress and stress reactions are very personal. It is, therefore, important to take the time to figure out oneself and one's personality so as to manage the situations one is likely to face and understand how one will react or respond to them.

I have discussed this subject in some detail, with data, to highlight to you that there are many aspects of life that cannot be avoided. They, however, can and do need to be managed. This can be done through realization, acceptance and, of course, effort. The rest of this book is precisely about this important aspect of management of stress that should lead us to happiness.

Suicide

In the context of happiness, success and stress, there is one other area I will address—suicide. This is one more unfortunate aspect of our life today. India, with 17 per cent of the world population, accounts for 20 per cent of suicides in the world. The rate of suicide in India has gone up, from 6.3 per 10,000 of population in 1978 to 8.9 in 1990 and 11.2 in 2011, a 77 per cent increase from 1978, despite all positive measures of growth and prosperity.[12] Suicide attempts tend to be up to twenty times more frequent than completed suicides. With all the progress the country has made, materially and economically, one would expect that people should be happier and there should be less reason for them to take the extreme step of self-harm by ending their lives. The reality, however counter-intuitive it may be, is that suicide is becoming a serious problem in the world. More tragically, this is now getting to be even more worrisome as it has increased not just among adults but even among people as young as in their early teens. Suicide, again, is closely linked to stress, and hence to happiness.

Search for Meaning Rather than Success

A final thought on the subject of success and happiness. There seems to be general agreement on one more factor that contributes to happiness—having meaning or purpose in one's life.

Viktor Frankl was an Austrian psychologist who managed to survive three years in German concentration camps in the Second World War but lost his family in the holocaust. As a result of his experience, he developed a school of psychotherapy called logotherapy. Logotherapy was recognized as the third school of Viennese psychotherapy after the first school by Sigmund Freud and the second by Alfred Adler. He postulated that life is primarily not a quest for pleasure as Freud believed or a quest for power as per Adler, but a quest for meaning. The great task is to find a meaning in life. His book *Man's Search for Meaning* about his years in the concentration camps is considered a classic in this field. To quote from the preface: 'Don't aim at success—the more you aim at it and make it a target, the more you are going to miss it. For success, like happiness, cannot be pursued; it must ensue, and it only does so as the unintended side-effect of one's dedication to a cause greater than oneself.'

Happiness, as we have seen earlier, is a state of contentment. Meaning is a more comprehensive sense of purpose and relates to the feeling of contributing to something greater than yourself.

> Humans may resemble many other creatures in their striving for happiness, but the quest for meaning is a key part of what makes us human, and uniquely so. – *Roy Baumeister et al*

> He who has a Why to live for can bear almost any How. – *Nietzsche*

To Sum Up

In this chapter we have gone into the domain of philosophy and a little bit of psychology to discuss happiness, success, stress and the meaning of life. We will see in the coming chapters that stress, mental health, clarity on what success means and the difference between pleasure and happiness are related to achievement of the ultimate goal of happiness. In the world we live in today, we can say with some definitiveness that happiness is not going to happen as a matter of routine or by default. Despite the tremendous progress that has been made—by material standards—in the recent past, we have seen that happiness cannot be taken for granted. As I see it, one has to work on achieving happiness.

We are living in an age of contradictions. We seem to have

More material comforts	but	Less happiness
More choice	but	Less satisfaction
More opportunities	but	More stress
More medical advances	but	More medical spend

In the next chapter we will take a look at what is happening in the world around us that makes happiness a difficult target for many. We will identify potential obstacles and roadblocks in our path to happiness. This will move us towards defining our GPS for finding the solution to happiness—the five I's.

3

THE WORLD TODAY: THE PRESSURE TO PERFORM

IN THE LAST CHAPTER we looked at what happiness and success are all about and the factors that might affect our achieving them. We also saw that data seems to point to the fact that material success and physical comforts are not necessarily making the world a happier place to be in. In this chapter we will see what is happening around us in the world today and the implications and impact it has on our ultimate goal of Happiness and Success.

As we saw in the last chapter, our world has been changing at a rate that is unbelievable and unimaginable for people like me, and probably for anyone over fifty years old. This would be true even for younger people. If you are Gen Y, it is highly unlikely that you had a smartphone in school. If you are Gen X, then you definitely did not possess even a mobile phone, let alone a smartphone!

Over the last fifteen years or so, the world has been turned upside down through disruptive innovations on various fronts. The smartphone, the advancements in telecommunications, the internet, e-commerce, social media, data mining, artificial intelligence and technologies have changed the way we live. The three big social media apps listed below would not have been even concepts just two decades ago. In a short span of less than fifteen years, up to 30 per cent (2 billion-plus people) of the world cannot do without these apps on an almost daily basis. These apps, amongst many other innovations, have changed the social fabric of life for all of us.

	Year established	**No. of users**	**Daily users**
Facebook (1)	2004	2.7 billion	1.6+ billion
WhatsApp (2)	2009	2.0 billion	500+ million
Instagram (3)	2010	1.0 billion	500+ million

Interestingly, India has the highest number of Facebook and WhatsApp users in the world.

We are living in a hugely connected world. The rate at which these ideas and many others have diffused and the wealth they have made for their founders are the envy of many. These rates of diffusion into the social system would have been unthinkable just a couple of decades ago. With all these amazing developments and phenomenal improvements in material comforts and almost unlimited opportunities for people, the world should be a happier place live in. Yet, as we saw in the last chapter, over the years happiness levels among populations have in fact been reducing, and stress levels have been on the increase. Studies show that current generations of all age groups are less happy than their earlier generations. The table below shows the mental health situation of various generations, according to a 2019 study by American Psychology Association.[4] This is what you, dear reader, have to watch out for—you are vulnerable, whether you are Gen X or Y.

Generation	Born between	Report good mental health	Have taken therapy
Baby boomers	1946–1962	70 %	15 %
Gen X	1961–1981	51 %	26 %
Gen Y	1981–1995	56 %	35 %
Gen Z	1995–2012	45 %	37 %

If the trends of the last few years are any indication of things to come, it is clear that happiness and emotional well-being cannot be taken for granted just because overall material comforts are increasing. It is obvious that a conscious effort will have to be made by you to ensure that you do not become one more victim to add to the statistic of people seeking therapy.

In order to find a solution, we first need to define the problem and understand the why and what of the situation before prescribing the how to solve it. In this section we will look at what is happening in the world around us that is leading to the present situation of concern—the why and the what. We will then look at the ways of dealing with these concerns.

The World of Sports and Life

The world of sports has a lot to teach us about life, success, achievement, goals, targets and so on. Today it is a world of heavy competition where anyone can win without the backing of money or position, and where the pay-outs in terms of money, fame and recognition are huge. This is a world where the euphoria of success can be as stressful as the pain of failure. I think it would be fair to say that almost everyone has contact with some sport or the other, and therefore the sports world will not be a completely alien context to any reader.

So here goes. I give below some snatches from the international sports domain. I would urge you to look at the examples and see what your takeaway is in the context of what we have discussed so far on success and happiness, working towards which is the ultimate purpose of this book.

2009 World Athletic Championships: Results of the 110m Men's Hurdles Finals

Rank	Name	Country	Timing (seconds)
1	Ryan Brathwaite	Barbados	13.14
2	Terrence Trammell	USA	13.15
3	David Payne	USA	13.15
4	William Sharman	Great Britain	13.30
5	Maurice Wignall	Jamaica	13.31
6	Peter Svoboda	Czech	13.38
7	Dwight Thomas	Jamaica	13.56
8	Ji Wei	China	13.57

2016 Olympics Championships: Results of the 100m Men's Free Style Finals

Rank	Name	Country	Timing (seconds)
1	Kyle Chalmers	Australia	47.58
2	Peter Timmers	Belgium	47.80
3	Nathan Adrian	USA	47.85
4	Santo Condorelli	Canada	47.88
5	Duncan Scott	Great Britain	48.01
6	Caeleb Dressel	USA	48.02
7	Cameron Mcevoy	Australia	48.12
8	Marcelo Chierighini	Brazil	48.41

2001 Wimbledon Men's Singles Finals

Player		Points won	Prize money	World ranking
G. Ivanasevic	Winner	154	$750,000	125
P. Rafter	Runner-up	150	$375,000	15

2012 ATP World Tour Finals, London

Player		Points won	Prize money
N. Djokovic	Winner	96	$1.24m
R. Federer	Runner-up	95	$0.41m

2015 US Open Championship Men's Singles Finals

Player		Points won	Prize money
N. Djokovic	Winner	147	$3.3m
R. Federer	Runner-up	145	$1.6m

Sports Earnings

The world of sports has become a big-bucks industry for the really successful sportspeople. The tables above give us an idea of the prize money in major tennis tournaments. The earnings of sportspeople typically come from two sources—prize money and endorsements. A sample of the earnings of some of the leading sportspersons for 2019 in different sports is given below:[5,6]

Name	Sport	Endorsement	Prize money	Total earnings
Roger Federer	Tennis	$100m	$6.3m	$106.3m
Tiger Woods	Golf	$60m	$2.3m	$62.3m
Virat Kohli	Cricket	$21m	$4m	$25.0m

What Are the Lessons?

As I look at these examples above, my belief is reinforced as to how we can take some simple and yet very powerful lessons from these events and adopt them as important insights in our personal lives. What do the numbers above tell you? I will tell you what they tell me and leave you to arrive at your own learnings.

Lesson 1: We are living in a world of intense competition.

a) In athletics and swimming, performance is measured by one's timing in the races. We can see from the examples above that the difference between the No. 1 and No. 8 athletes in a race is almost non-existent. For the more mathematically inclined, we can translate the difference in percentage terms. The difference between the timings of No. 1 and No. 8 is 3.2 per cent in the 2009 hurdles event and just 1.7 per cent in the 2016 swimming event. In fact, the difference in timing between athletes 1 and 2 is 0.005 per cent in the hurdles event and 0.46 per cent in the swimming event.

b) Moving over to tennis, we see that the scene there is not very different. If the number of points won is an indication of performance, the differences between the winner and the runner-up in these tournaments, over a time span of fifteen years, is 1.3 per cent in 2001, 0.5 per cent in 2012 and 0.7 per cent in 2015.

c) One other interesting point from the 2001 Wimbledon championship: Goran Ivanisevic, ranked No. 125 in the world, beat Patrick Rafter, ranked No. 15, at 110 places above him. It is anyone's victory on a day, irrespective of your ranking, position or reputation. Nothing can be taken for granted.
d) Things are continuing in the same momentum in almost every sport. If anything, the competition has become even more intense over the years, as can be seen from the results.

What we see from these examples from sports is that in world-class competition there is virtually no difference between the players across the spectrum and the competition is hyper-intense.

Shift to our world. It means that in every sphere of our life we are going to be pitted against hundreds if not thousands of people who are as good as us if not better. This competition starts in school, through college and university, and continues into our chosen professional fields. I am not referring to the corporate or business world alone. Look around in the world of music, art, sports, technology, science, education—anywhere. The race to be at the top is intense. To get to the top is demanding. To stay at the top is even more challenging. Unfortunately, in today's world, to get there and remain there seems to be a never-ending race.

The world of commerce is not very different. Look at automobiles, consumer durables, non-durables, services, consultancy, technology. All industries are flooded with brands and products that are as good as one another.

- Nike, Adidas, Reebok
- Honda, Toyota, Audi, BMW, Mercedes

- Taj, Oberoi, Welcomgroup
- Apple, Dell, Lenovo
- Infosys, WIPRO, TCS, Cognizant, Accenture, IBM

We can go on and on. Can we say any one brand of shoe is far better or worse than the other? Or any brand of car, hotel, computer or software company better than their competition? No, we cannot. The reality is that for the buyer they are all virtually commodities, irrespective of the nature of the product or industry. Every company, product or brand has to compete with others between whom there is little to choose from. It is exactly the same for us as individuals.

Implication: Success is extremely difficult to come by. The challenge is, how does one stand out in a world of clones. In today's world of competition, there is no player in any sport who can take the next match for granted. It really does not matter what your world ranking is. As they say, you are only as good as your last match. The difference between No. 1 and No. X is almost non-existent.

We can extend this to any sphere of life. Schools, colleges and organizations can pick from any number of people who are as brilliant, capable and intelligent as you are. In the workplace, you have to constantly compete against peers for recognition and promotion. It is not different in the world of art, music, literature and cinema either.

In short, success will never come easy and cannot be taken for granted.

Lesson 2: Where is the competition? The world is our battlefield.

Today competition cuts across all borders and boundaries. An athlete from a small country like Barbados or Jamaica can take on athletes from bigger and more powerful countries like America, China or

Great Britain. The universe we are competing with is not restricted to our proximate geographical environment.

The world is our battlefield. Thanks to the internet and communications and technology moving by leaps and bounds, competition and its impact are not restricted to one's neighbourhood, be it one's city, district, state or even country. To this extent, the implications of competition are more severe. Whether it is a student seeking admission to a leading university, a person seeking a job, or a product or service seeking acceptance and market share, the competition can come from any part of the world. Internet technologies and platforms allow access to people in the most remote parts of the world, both on the supply and demand sides. An American student seeking admission in a leading American university has to contend with students not only from New York but also students from Boston to Beijing. At leading universities in the world, the competition for a prospective recruit at prized organizations comes from all over the world too. A top college student in India is not just competing with her classmates or with students from other top colleges in India. Her competition comes from students from across Ivy League colleges the world over.

In the same way, a buyer can get access to suppliers anywhere in the world in both business-to-business (B2B) and business-to-customer (B2C) domains. This makes it that much more difficult for all the suppliers in that domain, because oftentimes the seller would not even know who the competition is. It is, of course, true that opportunities also open up for the seller. A student can access universities the world over, as can a job aspirant positions and a supplier buyers anywhere in the world. But then, the competition is also that much more. This situation applies to any profession, from music and the arts to farming and sports.

Implication: There are no borders when it comes to people who can challenge me. This makes the playing field that much larger. As we have seen earlier, given the fact that we are living in a world of clones as far as performance is concerned, the path to success gets even more tough and uncertain.

Lesson 3: An unfair world? The mismatch between reward and performance.

If we look at the earnings of leading sportsmen, we see the numbers are huge by any standard. Sports has become a high-earning industry. Look at the break-up of earnings of these sportsmen. We find that a significant portion of the annual earnings of these sportsmen actually comes from endorsements. It was about 85 per cent for Virat Kohli, and high as 94 per cent for Roger Federer.

Now look at the link between performance and reward. In the tennis situation, in the 2012 US Open Championship, for 2-point difference over 292 points played (2/292 = 0.7 per cent) the prize money difference is as high as 100 per cent. The winner gets 100 per cent more than the runner-up in prize money for winning just 2 points more. The situation is not different in 2015. You will find very similar situations in almost all sports. For an almost negligible difference in performance the difference in rewards is disproportionate. This does not seem okay, does it?

The real world is not different from the world of sports. Let's link these two worlds and see what we can take away. In the real world, too, rewards are not always reflective of actual performance, potential or effort. It does not seem fair. But this is the harsh reality of life and of the world of business. A fractional percentage point in an entrance exam can be the difference between an Ivy League education and a run-of-the-mill college course; between a job in a blue-chip company and somewhere else; between an order gained leading to a promotion and an order lost resulting in a pink slip.

Implication: The downside of failure and loss can be high.

Lesson 4: The stakes to win are high.

When you look at the earnings of leading sportspeople, two things stand out. Firstly, the annual earnings of the top people are really huge. Secondly, and interestingly, a substantial portion of their earnings comes from endorsements. As we see above, as much as 90 per cent of their annual earnings come from endorsements, appearances and the like, and only 10 per cent of their earnings from prize money. Remember, the player is in demand for endorsements that guarantee large sums of money only when the player is successful. This means he wins matches. The pressure on the player to win is thus very high. Take this analogy to the world of education or commerce, and it is no different. Winning is very difficult in today's world, for reasons explained above. Yet, the only measure of success is winning—getting high marks, getting into the right college, the right job, achieving the right numbers of revenue, growth, market share, market cap, and so on and on. The cost of losing is high.

Implication: This race is only getting to be more difficult with time and the stakes are increasing by leaps and bounds year after year. The 2001 Wimbledon champion took home $0.75m. The 2019 champion took home $2.98m. The prize money has quadrupled in twenty years. *The pressure and temptation to do anything to win can be high.*

We Want to Take the Elevator, Not the Stairs

Where does all of this leave us? In today's highly competitive world, it is becoming increasingly difficult to even qualify for a race, let alone win it. The pressure to perform continually and consistently is high. The stakes are high and the cost of losing is even higher. I see three things happening to us as a result.

Firstly, expectation levels keep going up. Everyone wants to be in the big league because that is what success is all about. The race starts from pre-school admission and ends many years later if it ends at all. We get caught in the crossfire of the pressure to both perform and conform. The need to keep up with the Joneses is high. An individual's performance, and consequently the perception of his or her success, is most often defined relative to others and not in absolutes. Unfortunately, oftentimes the expectations are not tempered by an objective assessment of personal potential and capability.

Secondly, as a result of this mode of judging people, our anxiety levels go up and tolerance levels go down. We want quick results—promotions, pay rises, bonuses, material comforts. These results again are benchmarked against those of our colleagues and even friends and acquaintances. I find my classmate from college who was not as bright as me doing much better than me financially in another company and I get upset. My satisfaction with my current assignment and boss diminishes, and I start looking for a new job. Promiscuity is the name of the game in the job market. The head-hunters, of course, act as the catalyst—showing people the carrot.

Thirdly, the environment only complicates matters. In many of the top B-schools and other leading institutions, prospective recruiters woo students and fall over each other to get the so-called top layer of students by fighting for the first-day slots at campus interviews. Many companies also offer joining bonuses. For many young students not yet out of college and with no real track record on the job or work experience, this kind of a situation results in their thinking they are really big cats. This also puts pressure on them to perform and justify the expectations of their recruiters and their own sense of personal worth.

From the large number of interactions I've had with students over the years, I find that among the current generation, frustration sets in faster. A look at the corporate world tells us that the pressure to perform is almost continuous, with daily, weekly, monthly, quarterly and annual targets to be achieved. It just goes on and on. The sole objective seems to be to get to the destination of achieving targets. No one has time to enjoy the journey any longer. Arriving at the destination has become all-consuming. Everyone is in a hurry to move ahead. I once heard a speaker put it across very well:

> No one wants to take the stairs. Everyone wants to use the elevator.

When we take the elevator, we do get to our destination faster but we miss out on the fun of the journey on the stairs. Sometimes we get to the destination and wonder what we are doing there.

As a golfer I can relate to this aspect very easily. Golf can be played by walking the full course or by taking a golf cart, which is faster and less exhausting. Ask any golfer and they will tell you that the fun and joy one gets in golf by walking can never be had by doing the rounds in a cart. After each shot, the real charm of golf is the walk to the ball where you have to hit the next shot. As you walk towards the ball you get time to take in the course, the environment and the surroundings. The walk up to the ball also gradually gives you a perspective as to how to hit the next shot. You get a better sense of what the next shot entails, and this allows you to select the right club and plan the shot.

In real life too I don't think it is any different. In our anxiety and hurry to reach a destination we miss out on the journey. Our pit stops are our targets, be they grades in school, results in entrance exams or weekly, monthly, quarterly targets at work. One target gets over and the next one kicks in. This is one treadmill we are on—never ending and never easing off. In the process, we neither have the time nor the inclination to make the effort to soak in the various facets of the travel and enjoy the journey.

In very simple terms in our context, amongst many other things this results in two outcomes:

- high stress levels among people at all stages of life,
- the resort to undesirable means—shortcuts, cheating—to achieve the end.

Neither of the above is desirable, and it is against these outcomes that one has to guard since they are obstacles to the final goal—Happiness. A corporate speaker I heard gave a very sound piece of advice to the young and impatient:

Deserve before Desiring,
Demonstrate before Demanding.

I am sure this needs no further explanation.

What is the solution?

We need to get people to take the stairs instead of the elevator. We need to somehow enjoy the journey and not make reaching the destination an end in itself. But how do we do it? This is a question I ask of my students as part of my final lecture. The answer is actually simple. Make the journey fun. When we enjoy doing what we are doing then it is no burden or chore. It's plain fun. A fun thing is something we look forward to. A fun thing is what we want to and like to do. Unfortunately for most of us, this will not happen in an obvious, natural manner. We will have to work at it. We will have to condition ourselves to seek the positive, the fun, in what we are doing. We will discuss these issues in the coming pages as a part of the GPS to happiness.

To Sum Up

We are living in a very fast-moving, competitive world. We need to take the time to stand back and think about where we want to head.

- What are the implications of what we have discussed in this chapter and the way the world is moving?
- What happens to us without our realizing it?
- Where can this leave us if we are not careful?

These are important issues to ponder on so that we do not lose our way on our journey. In the next chapter we will look at what has happened to people and organizations as a result of their falling prey to the realities of the situations we have seen in this chapter. That will lay the foundation for us to chart our journey through the 5 I's GPS.

4

THE WORLD TODAY: WINNING AT ALL COSTS

WE ARE LIVING IN A WORLD of intense competition and rapid change. There is continuous pressure on us to perform, achieve and succeed. The rewards of success are often disproportionate to the effort and performance behind the success. The stakes are big and the cost of failure is often high. As a result, success becomes an end in itself. The need to win becomes almost obsessive. We have touched upon some of the effects of this need to win and its impact on the overall health of an individual. In this context it is extremely important to keep a sense of perspective and clarity as to what one really wants to achieve and what the costs and benefits associated with the achievements will be.

In this chapter we will look at what happens to many of us as we move along in our journey of life. We will see what drives us to be successful. We work hard to get to our destination. When we get there, we want to be sure we have got to where we wanted. We often see people reaching their stated destination and then wondering what they are doing there. In fact, some of us end up in destinations we would never have dreamt we would. In the next few pages we will go through brief stories of well-known people and organizations. The people are normal folk, like you or me, who I am sure would never have dreamt they would end up where they did. Let us take a few pages out of their lives and see what we can learn from them.

Successful, Yes! But Happy?

Here are brief sketches of five people who hit the headlines both for the right and wrong reasons.

Rajat Kumar Gupta, Indian American executive

- Alumnus of IIT Delhi and Harvard Business School.
- Managing Director of management consultancy firm McKinsey & Company from 1994 to 2003, first foreign-born person to hold the post at the company.
- Board member of top corporations, including Goldman Sachs, Procter & Gamble and American Airlines.
- Adviser to non-profits such as the Bill and Melinda Gates Foundation and The Global Fund to Fight AIDS, Tuberculosis and Malaria.
- Founder of the Indian School of Business.
- Role model for aspiring Indians and young leaders.

Jeffrey Skilling, CEO, Enron Corporation

- Harvard Business School MBA.

- Graduated in the top 5 per cent of his class in 1979.
- One of the youngest partners in the history of McKinsey.
- In the year 2000, as CEO, oversaw Enron, with a revenue of about $100 billion and market capitalization exceeding $60 billion.
- Enron was rated the most innovative large company in America in Fortune's Most Admired Companies survey every year from 1996 to 2001.

David Petraeus, General, US Army

- Director of Central Intelligence Agency (CIA).
- Graduated as distinguished cadet of the United States Military Academy in the top 5 per cent of his class.
- Top graduate of the US Army Command and General Staff College in the class of 1983.

Lance Armstrong, Former American professional road-racing cyclist

- Survived cancer.
- Record seven-time winner of the Tour de France between 1999 and 2005. (The Tour de France is described as 'the world's most prestigious and most difficult bicycle race'. The event is a 3,630-km race of twenty-one long stages over the course of twenty-three days.)

Hanse Cronje, Captain, South Africa cricket team, 1990s

- Captained South Africa in a record fifty-three Tests and 138 One-Day International matches.

- One of the most successful captains in the world of cricket.
- Voted the eleventh greatest South African in 2004.

The five people profiled above have two things in common.

They reached the top in their respective careers. By any conventional definition, these people were extremely successful in their chosen fields of work or career. But they all went out in disgrace and disrepute.

Rajat Gupta: In 2012, he was sentenced to two years in prison after being found guilty of passing confidential boardroom information about Goldman Sachs to the Sri Lankan-American hedge fund manager Raj Rajaratnam. Gupta served nineteen months in prison.

Jeffrey Skilling: In 2000, under Skilling's stewardship, Enron was involved in a major accounting scandal that resulted in the largest bankruptcy ever to that date. In 2006, he was convicted of federal felony charges and sentenced to twenty-four years in prison.

David Petraeus: Resigned from his position as director of the CIA citing an extramarital affair with Paula Broadwell, an Army Reserve officer who had been writing his biography. In 2015, prosecutors recommended bringing felony charges against Petraeus for allegedly providing classified information to Broadwell while serving as director of the CIA.

Lance Armstrong: In 2012, he was stripped of all his titles over the biggest doping scandal in cycling history. It was found that Armstrong had used performance-enhancing drugs over the course of his career. He also received a lifetime ban from all sports that follow the World Anti-Doping Code.[1]

Hanse Cronje: In April 2000, Cronje was sacked as captain of the South African cricket team on charges of match-fixing activities. Cronje was banned from playing or coaching cricket for life. Cronje was killed in a private plane accident in 2002.

The common thread in all these stories—sad endings to brilliant people and high achievers.

This tendency is not restricted to individuals alone. Let us look at some large organizations.

Volkswagen, 2015: Defeat device brings $ 33 Billion in fines

In 2015, Volkswagen admitted to manipulating 11 million vehicles worldwide to fool emissions tests. VW cars sold in America had a 'defeat device'—or software—in diesel engines that could change test results to show improved performance. The result? The engines emitted nitrogen oxide pollutants up to forty times above what is allowed in the US. Volkswagen admitted to the cheating. This scandal cost Volkswagen over $ 33 billion in fines, compensation and legal costs.

Martin Winterkorn, chairman of Volkswagen, chairman of the supervisory board of Audi and chairman of the board of management of Porsche Automobil Holding SE, had to resign. Winterkorn was criminally indicted over the emissions cheating scandal in the United States on 3 May 2018 on charges of fraud and conspiracy. In April 2019, he was criminally indicted on charges of fraud in Germany.

Wells Fargo, 2016: Fake accounts lead to $3 billion in fines[2]

From 2002 to 2016, employees of Wells Fargo used fraud to meet impossible sales targets. They opened millions of accounts in customers' names without their knowledge, signed unwitting account holders up for credit cards and bill-payment programmes, created fake personal identification numbers, forged signatures and even secretly transferred customers' money. The US government fined Wells Fargo $3 billion to settle criminal civil action liabilities. John Stumpf, chairman of the bank and a career banker, had to resign following this scandal.

Ranbaxy, 2005: Falsification of records, $500 million in fines[3]

Ranbaxy was found to have committed fraud by submitting 'untrue statements'. The Food and Drug Administration in the US found that Ranbaxy had a 'persistent' 'pattern' of submitting 'untrue statements'. On at least fifteen new generic drug applications, auditors found more than 1,600 data errors. This meant their drugs were 'potentially unsafe and illegal to sell'.

General Motors, 2013: Irregularities in the automaker's emission-testing programmes in India[4]

GM reportedly admitted that GM employees wilfully faked emissions inspections so its vehicles could pass standards. Sam Winegarden, GM's vice president for global engine engineering, was fired, along with about ten other GM Powertrain employees in the US and India.

Why? Why? Why? Other Corporate Frauds

- Theranos, 2018, USA: approximately $9 billion in overvaluation[5]
- Danske Bank, 2018, Denmark: $234 billion in money laundering[5]
- Nirav Modi, 2017, India: $2 billion bank fraud[5]
- Olympus, 2011, Japan: $1.7 billion accounting fraud[6]
- MDB Malaysia, 2018: $4.5 billion in money laundering[7]

The five organizations named here constitute a very small sample from the list of organizations that have been involved in frauds, scams and scandals in recent years. The list goes on and on, over years and across the world. Almost all the senior people involved in these activities are likely in jail currently or fighting criminal cases. I have taken this small sample to demonstrate that it is evident that such events are not limited to any one part of the world or society. The corporate and political worlds are graveyards of large organizations and powerful individuals who have succumbed to probably mankind's oldest failings—temptation and greed. I always wonder why people do things that seem clearly inappropriate and illegal even to a casual observer! What happens to people and organizations? What is it that makes these people stake their years of sweat and hard work, their reputation and standing, to bring them to such avoidable ends?

Large corporations get sucked into it as much as individuals do. Of course, corporations are only made up of people, so it should not be totally surprising. The cause for concern when fraud is organizational is that the whole system becomes part of the process. The five cases listed here are only representative of a malaise that exists in our society. Do an internet search of scams, scandals and frauds, and you can spend a considerable amount of your time on it. I would urge you to read up on these and other cases to get a sense of the magnitude of the problem and what can happen if we are not clear about ourselves and our destination. Reports and books on these people and companies will make for fascinating reading, if nothing else, and give you a lot to think about. Many books have been written and movies made on corporate scams and scandals around these and other examples.

The purpose of this book is not to analyse such people and situations. Neither do I want to pontificate on what is good and bad, right and wrong, moral and immoral. There are enough people in the world making a living doing this. What I see as an alert or red flag is for us to understand that these situations can happen to the best of us. You do not have be an inherently devious person from childhood to end up doing these seemingly stupid things. The lesson for me is simple. If it can happen to these people and organizations, it can happen to me also. Do I want to end up like them? If not, then what can I do to ensure that I do not fall into a similar trap?

I often wonder what happens during the journey these people made towards success and happiness. What made these people do what they did? As I think about it, what I realize is that people do not land up in such situations suddenly one day. There is no equivalent of a Eureka moment in such instances. These situations happen gradually over a period of time. You don't realize the implications of the changes happening to your personality, attitudes and behaviour. Or, when the priorities and perspectives of success consume you to the extent of blinding you to the repercussions of your actions. That precisely is the danger. Things happen to us without our realizing it, and before we even get to know, it is often too late.

The examples I have taken above are not outliers or rare exceptions. We hear of such cases almost every day of the year. I have chosen these examples because each one of the individuals listed was a high achiever. They were not inherently bad people. They would have been in the top of their pack wherever they were—in school, in college, in their organizations, in their chosen professions. They would have been the envy of their peers and the darlings of their bosses, coaches, mentors. The organizations I have named are, again, all leaders in their own right. Their reputations have been built painstakingly and slowly over years by the predecessors of the fallen leaders. The people heading these organizations are also leaders of great standing and have contributed much to their organizations.

Let us go back in time to their lives when they were in their late teens or early twenties. During discussion time in my class I would ask the question—when these people were in college or in their early years of work, if they were told that fifteen or twenty years down the road they would end up in jail or in ignominy, what would have been their reaction? The unanimous response is that they would have laughed and dismissed it with an 'Are you serious? Me? No way.' They would have sworn that there is no way they would go down the path of dishonesty and cheating. I am sure they would have said it in all seriousness and meant every bit of it.

What happens to us unknowingly over the years in our journey to success? This is not a treatise on human psychology or social dynamics. I keep it simple—what happens to us, and why? How can I ensure I am happy in the end? There may be many triggers that spur us in our journey towards success. Two of them are:

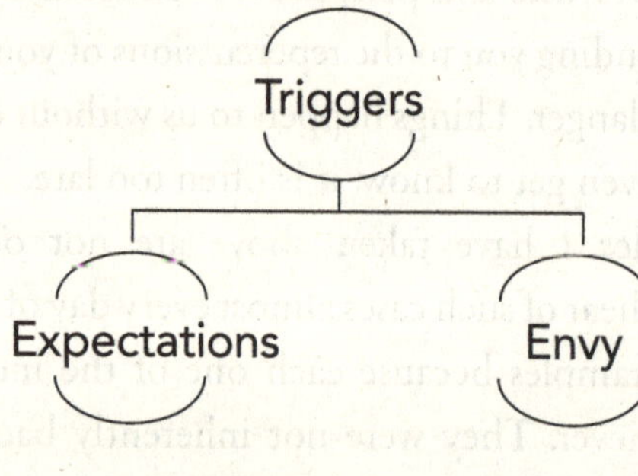

Expectations. Envy. Two things that can drive us or destroy us. By themselves they are not bad. In fact, we need them to do something meaningful. As we have seen earlier, human beings need a sense of meaning in their lives. When expectations and envy result in greed, hunger for power and arrogance, then we have a problem. And, of course, we have unhappiness!

Expectations

We all have expectations. We need expectations, or else we will be vegetables. Expectations help us set goals and targets to achieve. They drive us to perform. The issue is management of expectations, and that is where the delicate balance kicks in. We do not want to nurse expectations that are too low and do not do justice to our potential. We also do not want to harbour expectations that are too high, too unrealistic and compel us to choose undesirable paths to achieve them.

How do expectations typically get set? What can we do to have realistic expectations? We need to give this some thought.

Expectations can be triggered by external or internal stimuli.

We want to be like others, and thus what they have or what they do set our expectation levels. We are also often pushed by others to do something. I am sure many of us have experienced pressure in some form or the other from our parents in our growing-up years. This comes in the form of:

- Comparisons with other kids or siblings—'see how your classmate is doing'; 'why can't you be like your sister?'
- Commands—'I expect you to study for engineering'; 'you don't know how lucky you are, if only I had these opportunities when I was your age'; 'we are a family of lawyers, you have to continue this tradition'.
- Subtle messages—'when I was your age I would . . . ', 'I have done it, you can too if only you applied your mind to this'; 'you have the potential'; 'look at the amount of sacrifices we have made for you . . .'

As we grow older, pressure could come from our partner or spouse. This would of course come as a result of their own aspirations and expectations. The common manifestation of this is the 'keeping up with the Joneses' syndrome, which may also be your individual trigger too.

Internal triggers are equally important. They come from your own demands on yourself and how you define success. Unfortunately, from our childhood we are conditioned to evaluate personal success through external benchmarks. My happiness depends on what the other person does or gets. I get a hike of 12 per cent in my salary. The average hike in the company is 8 per cent. I should be happy and consider this as success. But my colleague gets a hike of 15 per cent. All of a sudden, I become unhappy!

The pressures condense into two forms: pressure to perform or pressure to conform. These pressures could result in a person feeling the need to achieve targets at any cost.

When the trigger is from within and the benchmark is set by comparing ourselves with or wanting what someone else has, we might get into one more trap—envy. Like expectations, envy can do as much good as it can harm, and it is worth spending some time discussing this.

Envy

Envy: painful or resentful awareness of an advantage enjoyed by another joined with a desire to possess the same advantage

One of the seven deadly sins as per Christian teachings is envy. Envy figures in almost all religions and mythologies and as the cause of wars and trouble in history. From the time of the Mahabharata and the Iliad a few thousand years ago to family feuds in the corporate world today, envy has been at the root of problems for and between people.

Envy is a universal and timeless phenomenon. Each of us must have experienced this emotion to some extent at some time in our lives. Like stress and expectations, envy has a role to play in our path to achievement. We need a trigger to drive us to set goals and perform. Like stress, envy is required in the right amount to help us in our performance. Too much of it and it is counterproductive. Even destructive. Envy is generally seen as a negative emotion, and we shall discuss it in this context and its impact on happiness.

At one level, it is only through some degree of envy that one can dream and help us have a concept of ourselves. Having others as benchmarks and seeking to be like them is where envy can play a powerful positive role. Envy—to want to be like someone else or have what others have—can act as a stimulant for our aspirations and goals. To this extent it can be a motivator and driver of achievement. However, like many other qualities and factors, if envy is not in the right amount or balance it can bring on unproductive results.

Let us look at some dimensions of envy and their harmful effects. Envy has three components:[8]

- Someone has something that you don't have.
- You want that something.
- Your not having it causes you pain or resentment.

Two out of three components of envy are within your control.

- You want that something that the other person has. Why?
- Not having it causes you pain. Why?

Ask yourself, when does something you don't have and others have cause you pain or resentment? We do not generally envy people we do not know. It is only when there is someone we know well and who has something we do not have that the element of pain comes in. Bertrand Russell said, 'Beggars do not envy millionaires, though of course they will envy other beggars who are more successful.'

To restate this concept—envy is directed at people whom we know and not at strangers. We are thus envious of our classmates, friends, neighbours, relatives and colleagues. We would not normally be envious of some stranger who is much better off than us. I might wish I had the success of Sundar Pichai for his achievements in the international corporate world, or the academic brilliance of a Nobel Prize winner or the talent of Roger Federer for his tennis mastery. The fact is, they all possess or did something that I could not. But does that cause me pain? No. I might say I envy them, but in true terms it is not really envy. On the other hand, my colleague buys himself a new fancy car thanks to his promotion. I envy him. That surely causes me pain—and a lot more than a billionaire businessman buying one. I wonder how that guy could get to doing it when I think I am much better than him and cannot aspire to become what he is and get what he has. In the first instance, we may say that the envy is passive or benign.

> Every time a friend succeeds, I die a little.
> – Gore Vidal

Since envy is generally directed at someone we know, one significant fallout is the effect it can have on relationships. It could affect the closest of relationships. We have numerous instances of fallouts between close friends, colleagues and even siblings because of envy.

I am sure all of us have knowledge of such instances both in our personal world and in the public domain.

Effects of Envy

The pain from envy, as in the case of stress, can have three effects on a person:

- Affect his or her emotional well-being—create frustration, anger, anxiety, depression, etc.
- Affect his or her behaviour—cause a person to sabotage or cause harm to the other person.
- Affect his or her physical health.

Envy could result in feelings of inferiority or inadequacy. Your self-respect can suffer as a result of the pain you feel at someone else's success. Since envy is triggered by someone close to you, it may not be possible to openly express your opinions and feelings to the people around you. We really do not come across someone who comes to you and says, 'I envy you for your talent and it makes me angry that you are so much better than me!' Because of the social stigma attached to envy, it is also difficult to talk about our feelings of envy and express our emotions to others. As a basic concept of stress management will tell you, one big cause of stress is inability to express our feelings openly. The need to conceal, disguise or deny our feelings of envy makes things worse. Going to an extreme, envy can result in one being disparaging of the person who is the object of envy—belittling or talking ill of him or her.[9]

One way of handling your emotions could also be to distance yourself from the person you envy. This, you hope, will reduce the pain of having to be reminded of the cause of your pain. The danger in envy lies in the old phrase—'being consumed with envy'. Some people become so fixated on a rival that they lose their focus on their own performance.

Having seen the effects of envy on the individual, it is easy to see how it can impact relationships, teamwork and organizational effectiveness. This is, of course, in addition to the possible harm it does to the individual suffering envy. Envy is difficult to manage, in part because it's hard to admit that we harbour such a socially unacceptable emotion. Our discomfort causes us to conceal and deny our feelings, and that makes things worse. Repressed envy inevitably resurfaces, stronger than ever.

To quote Rajat Gupta:

'When I look at it myself, yeah, I am driven by money. I like many creature comforts. I want to make sure I take care of my kids well and so on and so forth. And when you live in this society you do get fairly materialistic, so I look at that. I am disappointed. I am probably more materialistic today than I was before and I think money is very seductive . . . you have to watch out for it because the more you have it, you get used to comforts, and you get used to, you know, big houses and vacation homes, and going and doing whatever you want, and so it is very destructive. However much you say that you will not fall into the trap of it, you do fall into the trap of it.'

Yes, Rajat Gupta should know. Assessments of his net worth at the time of his case range between $100 million and $180 million.[10] Certainly not loose change.

Social media and increased connectivity, which characterize today's world, are other catalysts to add to our vulnerability to envy and the attendant stress it causes. Access to what happens to people in an ongoing manner gives greater avenues and opportunities for people to get carried away by envy.

When I look at my Facebook page, which, incidentally, is not very often, I wonder at the relevance of many posts on the platform. Why do people post some messages for the world at large—messages that seem to have little or no relevance to anyone except the person posting them? For example:

- 'Enjoying lovely strawberry and cream on the lawns of Wimbledon. Waiting for the Djoko Federer finals on centre court.'
- 'Lovely evening on the banks of the Seine. Enjoying the sunset and looking forward to Oktoberfest on the weekend.'
- 'Just got my new car. Was a toss-up between a Jaguar and a Maybach.'

Looking at these posts, I wish to tell them—why would I care whether you are eating strawberries in Wimbledon, pasta in Paris or *chaat* and *gol gappas* on Chowpatty? It's your life. Do what you want.

So, what are these people really trying to say? To my uncomplicated mind, what they are saying is, 'Eat your heart out guys. I have arrived and you thought I was a loser.'

The social media world is full of messages and status reports that add to our cup of woes in two ways:

- We get to know a lot of things about people whom we know and are in touch with, and it would have been nicer for us to not know about these things.
- We get updates about people with whom we had no contact for years, and suddenly we see what they are doing.

Remember, pain generally happens when the person causing it is known to us. So a Facebook post of Brad Pitt's from Wimbledon or Aamir Khan's from Paris is absolutely no problem for me. But what if the post is from my 'duh' classmate whom I haven't seen since college? Or my neighbour whom I think is so average? When I see their posts, the internal juices start flowing!

To Sum Up

In this chapter we have seen how we can get caught in the race to get ahead in a very competitive and demanding world. The pressure to win gets hold of many of us without any conscious intent, plan or strategy on our part. It just happens, even to the best of us.

Expectations and envy could be the starting points to get us thinking on our journey towards happiness and success.

By themselves expectations and envy are not bad, but they can be double-edged swords. It's their net effect by which one must evaluate their relevance and impact. They can either spur us to achievement and fulfilment, or blind us to reality and our unique capabilities. The challenge for us is to know how to harness their power and draw the fine line for expectations and envy to work favourably for us. They can then help us achieve and perform and yet not consume us in making our targets and goals ends in themselves.

Our expectations and our disposition towards envy and the kind of issues and events that trigger envy will change with age and time. It is good to take stock of our expectations and calibrate them with respect to our priorities and perspectives as we move along in life. We are not the same person at fifteen, twenty-five, thirty, forty, fifty and sixty years of age. Our goals keep changing, our priorities keep changing.

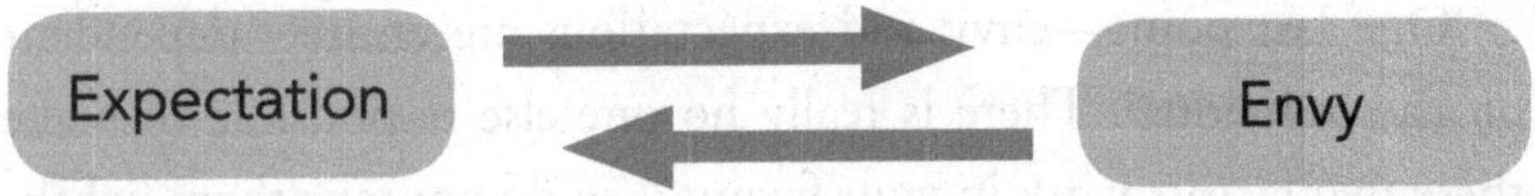

Expectations and envy are interlinked. Do expectations lead to envy? Or envy to expectations? I envy you so I have expectations. And I have expectations that lead to my envying you. It is the chicken-and-egg story.

Expectations and envy are also connected to our perception of success. Oftentimes, the measure of success is relative rather than absolute. I define or evaluate my success or failure based on the performance of others. This affects both the setting up of expectations and the level of envy experienced. As I have discussed in this chapter, we are often under pressure to perform and pressure to conform. Both these pressures could influence our expectations and the degree of envy we might experience. To help us get the right balance between the positive and negative impacts they can have, we could keep one more thought in mind. The degree of success we may achieve in any chosen field will depend on three broad factors:

- Competence
- Commitment
- Consistency

It will be useful to periodically calibrate yourself on these three parameters with respect to your desired or stated goals. It will also help you set goals that are adequately challenging and push you to your potential. Set reasonable expectations that match your capabilities, temperament and character.

One last point—envy and expectations are entirely dependent on the individual. There is really no one else responsible to make these two factors work in your favour—so do not take them lightly.

We have set a backdrop for what could be factors that block our path to Happiness and Success. In the next section I will discuss my formula for happiness and a meaningful life.

PART 2

5

THE 5 I's: A PERSONAL GPS TO HAPPINESS

In the first part of this book I have tried to lay a context to the relevance and importance of having a road map for life. We have so far looked at the following:

- **What** are we really trying to achieve in life—happiness or success?
- **What** is the situation that makes happiness elusive for many?
- **Why** is this happening despite all the progress made by mankind over the years?
- **What** are the possible roadblocks and obstacles we are likely to face in our journey towards happiness?

If there is any one point that needs to emerge clearly and needs to be reinforced constantly, it is this:

Happiness is not a natural consequence of success. Happiness will not happen by chance but will only be achieved by design and thought.

I have said it earlier, and at the risk of being repetitive I say it again. I am in no way preaching, moralizing or prescribing a formula. I have questioned myself at various points and evaluated my successes and failures, as also those of others known to me and of public figures. I have looked at myself and others and have tried to make sense of things in the context of happiness and the meaning of life. I have put together my experiences, my readings, learning and thinking about these aspects, and have tried to figure out the jigsaw puzzle that many of us are generally trying to solve in life. Over years, the pieces have fallen into place.

As any student of management will know, academicians like to present frameworks that are simple to understand and remember. We thus have:

- 4 P's of marketing
- 5 S's of housekeeping
- 3 C's of strategy
- 5 W's and 1 H of problem-solving

It is now time to see *how* we can get to our goal with:

The 5 I's to Happiness

The next five chapters in this section are my attempts to put the puzzle together for you. I call it my road map or GPS, if you will, for happiness and, consequently, success. Not the other way around. The five I's are, in a way, presented in an order of priority, though it is true that you need all these ingredients in the right proportion to achieve the goal of happiness. You may well see the five I's in a different order of priority. To each his or her own!

6

INTEGRITY: THE MORAL COMPASS

WE HAVE SEEN THAT the world of sports is a good place to learn some of life's lessons. In many ways, it simulates what the real world is all about—intense competition, high stakes, clear objectives to be achieved, general guidelines and rules that define what is acceptable and what is not. The player knows where she stands with respect to others at any point in time during the match through the score; there are referees who are essentially impartial to ensure the game goes on as required, and so on. I am going back to this domain for the first of the five I's of happiness.

Dishonesty Is Not Equal to Cheating

Let us take a small glimpse into the lives of four leading sportsmen:

1. G.R. Vishwanath (Vishy) was an outstanding Indian cricketer in the 1970s and early 1980s. He was considered one of the most stylish batsmen of his time. He did not make it to the

captaincy of the Indian team. His career largely overlapped with that of the 'little master', Sunil Gavaskar, who is also his brother-in-law. Vishy did, however, captain India in two Test matches. The first of these was the Golden Jubilee Test between England and India, played in Bombay (Mumbai) in 1980. England was reeling at a score of fifty-eight with five wickets down in the first innings. Bob Taylor the batsman edged a ball from Kapil Dev to the wicketkeeper. Taylor was given out by the umpire. Standing nearby at the slip position, Vishy was convinced that the ball had not taken the edge of the bat and the umpire was incorrect in his call. Viswanath asked Taylor whether he had nicked the ball and the English batsman replied in the negative. Vishwanath convinced the umpire to reverse the decision. Taylor was called back and continued his batting. India went on to lose the match.

2. Adam Gilchrist (Gilly), an Australian cricketer, was a flamboyant wicketkeeper and opening batsman. He was also the vice-captain of the Australian cricket team. In the 2003 World Cup Tournament, in a crucial semi-final match against Sri Lanka, Gilchrist tried to sweep the bowler but got an edge to his bat. The ball was caught by a fielder. The Sri Lankan appeal for a catch was ignored by the umpire, who ruled that the ball had only hit the pad. Gilchrist waited to hear the verdict. He then turned and walked back to the pavilion even though the umpire had ruled Gilchrist not out. Fortunately for Australia, they won the match and also went on to win the World Cup that year.
3. Andy Roddick is an American tennis player who held the world number one rank in 2003. Roddick was playing Fernando Verdasco of Spain in the round of sixteen at the Rome Masters 2005. In a best-of-three-sets match, Verdasco was one set down and 2-5 in the second set. He was now serving love-40 to

America's top player. For people not familiar with tennis, this would mean that Roddick was one point away from winning the match and had three match points. Verdasco's second serve was called out by the line judge. Roddick had effectively won the match. Roddick, however, told the umpire that Verdasco's serve had nicked the line and the serve was in fact good. Stunned, the umpire let Roddick overrule him. Verdasco fought back by holding the serve, winning the next few games to win that set and the next set, and to win the match itself.

4. Brian Davis is a golfer whom many golfers themselves would not have heard of. In the Verizon Heritage Golf Tournament in April 2010, Davis was in the reckoning for his first PGA TOUR title championship. He had a play-off with high-ranking golfer, Jim Furyk. The play-off in golf is the equivalent of a sudden death penalty shoot-out in a football match. The first player to win a hole wins the match, and in this case the championship too. On the first extra hole, Davis strayed into a hazard left of the green. As he took his backswing, he thought he had touched a loose reed on his backswing. This would amount to a foul attracting a penalty. Davis called the referee over for a judgement. The foul was not an obvious one, borne out by the fact that it was not pointed out by any spectator and could not be seen in normal video replays. The infringement could be seen only in slow-motion replays. A foul was confirmed after a lot of deliberation and many video replays. Davis immediately conceded victory to Furyk. In effect, Davis had called a two-shot penalty on himself that cost him a potential first PGA TOUR victory. In the process, he also had to settle for the runner-up cheque of $615,000 instead of the winner's cheque of $1.03 million. He gave up a possible $410,000 in earnings. 'I thought I saw movement out of the corner of my eye. And I thought we'd check on TV,' Davis said.

These are just a few of many similar examples we would find in the world of sports. I have taken these four since they cover sports over different time periods and different conditions. In these situations lies the basis of my discussions in my class on happiness, success and dilemmas when it comes to achievement of one's goals. Let's look at what these examples above point to and what we can learn from them. My discussions revolve around four questions.

Question 1. If the sportspeople in the examples above did not do what they did, that is, overrule the referee, could they be accused of cheating?

Question 2. If yes, why? If no, why not?

Question 3: Should the players have done what they did?

Question 4: Why did these players do what they did?

Here is my take and a brief summary of the typical discussions I have in my final lecture session in my courses.

Answer 1: The answer to this question in all my classes and seminars is a near-unanimous NO. The people in these examples could not have been accused of cheating if they did not ask the referees to overrule their own decisions.

Answer 2: Why can't they be accused of cheating? The answer is quite simple. It is the job of the referee and not the players to rule on points of law in the game. It is not the player's responsibility to tell the referee what to do. So, if Vishy, Gilly or Roddick did not overrule the umpire on a decision in their favour no one could really say that they were breaking the rules or doing something wrong.

Answer 3: This is the tough one. This results in a debate, with a majority of the students in my classes saying that what these players did was right. They were being honest and following their conscience. The answer to this question is, unfortunately, not that simple. We will discuss this a little later.

Answer 4: The four sportsmen displayed very high levels of sportsmanship. The word used to define their behaviour is integrity; the players displayed a high level of integrity.

If the players did not do what they did, they would not really be cheating but they would be dishonest to themselves. We see that there is a clear difference between being dishonest and being a cheat. So, what is the difference between being dishonest and cheating? Dishonesty is not being honest to oneself and one's set of principles and values. It is about answering to oneself and one's conscience. Cheating, on the other hand, is about breaking a framework of rules and guidelines that define the boundaries of acceptable and unacceptable actions and behaviour in a context, which could be social, organizational or professional.

RV says,

DISHONESTY ≠ CHEATING

On the flip side of the examples above, let's take another story that involves the Argentinian footballer Diego Maradona. Maradona is definitely amongst the all-time top ten of football greats. In the now infamous 1986 World Cup quarter final match against England, Maradona scored a goal which went off his hand. Maradona made no mention of it to the referee. The goal was awarded to Argentina. Argentina went on to win the match 2-1 and also the World Cup that year. That goal is infamously referred to as the 'hand of God' goal, quoting Maradona himself.

Was Maradona a cheat in not owning up to the referee? Was it his duty to own up to the hand goal or was it the referee's job to see it and call the foul? Maradona got a huge amount of criticism for that goal, but thirty-four years after the event the jury is still out on whether what he did was truly wrong. Ironically, Maradona also scored the second goal for Argentina, which is regarded as the goal of the century!

This brings us to our first **I—Integrity**.

Integrity—What's That?

There are various interpretations and contexts in which the word integrity is used to describe a certain quality possessed by a person, an object, an organization or a process. The quality generally has to do with the subject's honesty, trustworthiness or their living up to commitments and expectations. Integrity is an overused word in the corporate world as well as in the world of philosophers and spiritual leaders. This word appears in almost all corporate mission statements to define the organization, the people in the organization and the manner in which they will deal with all stakeholders. For this book I will stick to integrity in the context of a positive characteristic of an individual, since we are talking about the path to happiness and success for an individual, though the definition would apply just as well to organizations too.

The dictionary gives the following definitions of integrity:

- Firm adherence to a code of especially moral or artistic values: incorruptibility
- An unimpaired condition: soundness
- The quality or state of being complete or undivided: completeness

For our purposes we will lean on the first definition. In this context, integrity largely implies being honest and having strong moral principles. The key words are *honest*, *moral* and *principled.* Integrity is essentially a quality or characteristic of a person.

To translate integrity into something tangible and implementable is, however, a challenge. What was morally acceptable amongst the Egyptian royalty during Cleopatra's times in 50 BCE of a brother marrying his sister is shocking today. In fact, it is illegal since it amounts to incest. Closer to home, as recently as about seventy-five years ago, in almost every part of India it was very common for girls to get married at age thirteen or fourteen and have their first child before they were fifteen. Many people of my era, born in the 1940s and 1950s, would have had grandparents who would fall into this category. They were people from all rungs of society and not necessarily from illiterate, uneducated, traditional or conservative families and backgrounds. Today the legal age for marriage for women in India is eighteen years, though this law apparently gets flouted. Thus, what is illegal today was quite acceptable and normal just seventy years ago. Interestingly, in 2019 the Supreme Court of India held that sexual intercourse by a man with his wife who is below eighteen years of age is rape.[1]

Honesty, morality and principles are themselves subjective and are time-, place-, individual, situation- and culture-dependent. We will talk about it a little more as we end this book.

So, what is integrity? Essentially, integrity is about who you are and what defines you as a person. I believe integrity is that part of you that drives you as an individual and gives you clarity and direction when you have to make choices.

The best definition of integrity that I have come across is:

What you do when no one is watching.

Integrity is not so much about the outside world as much your inner person. Given the above definition, it is quite easy to understand why Vishy, Gilchrist, Roddick and Davis did what they did. They were not driven by the rules of the game as much as by their conscience. Conscience—this is the other word that is often linked to integrity. Conscience is essentially internal to a person. All of the sportspersons in the examples did what they did because of their conscience. They knew what had actually happened even if the others had not seen it. It was important for them to own up. I expect they uphold a quality that must be important to them—integrity.

Let's look at what the dictionary definition of integrity implies. The operating words are adherence, moral, values. In simple language, it is about sticking to principles. This would necessarily involve:

- Knowing the principles that are important to you.
- Others being aware of where you stand with respect to your principles—explicitly by statement or implied through your actions and behaviour.
- Actions that are consistent within those set of principles even when they are inconvenient to you.

It is nice to sing praises of integrity. People who demonstrate high levels of integrity are seen to be honest, respectful of rules, have sound values and are strong on moral principles. Their behaviour and actions, which align with their stated principles, make them appear trustworthy and reliable. These are certainly good qualities to have anywhere and at any time—in one's personal, professional or social life. In real life, things do not always work out to fit into one's scheme of principles and value systems. We have to make difficult choices, as Vishy, Gilchrist and Maradona had to. It is at these times that a person's level of integrity is tested. The challenge of being a person with integrity is to be consistent—an important quality to be reliable. This is easier said than done.

Integrity—Where Is the Problem?

Life is one continuous journey of problem-solving and conflict resolution. At different stages in our lives we will be faced with various options, which call for decisions. These could be as simple as 'should we do a Chinese dinner or Indian?', 'should I take the flight or the train', 'should I buy brand A or brand B', and so on. They could also be more complicated, like 'should I join institute A or B?', 'should I do this course or that', 'should I take this job or that', and so on.

There will be many occasions when we will have to make difficult decisions. All decisions are not obvious and easy to make. Decisions will have long- or short-term implications, and the stakes will vary. In most cases, the impact of the decisions will be known later, and one's ability to retract from or reverse one's decision may be limited, if not impossible. Many of these decisions may not have moral implications or repercussions, as we can see from the examples we have discussed. But what happens if you are in the position of the sportsmen? There is a matter of morality, conscience and honesty in their situations. And trade-offs.

This leads us to the next situation—managing trade-offs. Keep in mind that decision-making is invariably a matter of choosing between alternatives and thus making trade-offs. In a trade-off we give up something to get something. This is the challenge. When choosing between right and wrong, there is really no conflict. If you choose the wrong option, then you make a conscious decision knowing that what you are doing is wrong and ready to face the consequences. For example, when I jump a traffic light when there is no cop around, I know that what I am doing is inherently wrong, and there is really no intrinsic dilemma except to consider the options if I am caught.

The challenge is when you have to choose between two options, neither of which is really wrong and both are equally valid. Take Vishy or Gilchrist, for example. In the process of being people of strong integrity, they let down their team. The issue is very basic. To whom do we owe responsibility when we are part of a team, community or organization? Would the team have been okay with their decision to overrule the umpire?

From the team's perspective, Vishy should have stayed with the umpire's decision and not called Taylor back. That would have been part of a player's obligation to the larger cause of the team. On the other hand, calling him back would also be right, because consistency of behaviour is also important. Thus, there is really no correct decision.

In a situation like this, what does one do? At what stage does the team's interest get priority over individual principles and values? Did Vishy or Gilchrist do the right thing?

Interestingly this dilemma has been addressed in the Mahabharata, (Book 2, *Sabha Parva, Sisupala-badha Parva*, Section LXI), where the poet Sukra says:

> For the sake of a family a member may be sacrificed, for the sake of a village a family may be sacrificed, for the sake of a province a village may be sacrificed and for the sake one's own soul the whole earth may be sacrificed.

The guideline from the Mahabharata is clear. For the sake of a larger good, an individual's well-being may be sacrificed. However, when it comes to one's individual soul, then the earth may be sacrificed. This would imply that one's personal integrity takes preference over the larger good of the team. Given our context, it is clear that what Vishy and Gilchrist did was really the right thing. The team may not have been happy about it and may also not entirely agree with this point of view. The situation was not the same for Andy Roddick or Brian Davis. They were not playing a team game and were answerable only to themselves for their actions.

Let us look at another perspective from the military services. The Chetwode Motto engraved in the Indian Military Academy in Dehradun says:

> The safety, honour and welfare of your country come first, always and every time. The honour, welfare and comfort of the men you command come next. Your own ease, comfort and safety come last, always and every time.

Going by this motto, the team's interest is paramount and individual's comfort comes last.

We have two conflicting guidelines, both of which seem equally valid. Which one is right? If both are right, then which one should I follow? There is really no one who can answer this question except yourself.

Integrity—the Moral Compass

There is a conflict between what they believed was right as per their conscience or values and what would normally be expected by the team or from the rules of the game. The issue is not so much about what Vishy or Gilchrist should have done in their situations but how could they have lived with their decisions if what they did went against their conscience. This can happen if and only if they were clear about the priorities and trade-offs and their implications. We can see that there would have been a dilemma and a conflict situation for each player—should he own up to what he did wrong or let it be? From the actions of these players, it is very apparent that when it comes to matters of integrity and conscience, there is no thinking and evaluating the situation. The responses were almost instantaneous and instinctive. This can happen only if this characteristic is an integral part of a person's character. It is in times like this, of which there will be plenty in one's journey in life, that we need a framework to help us understand the trade-off implications and make the appropriate decision. The framework will help us evaluate our options and also the implications of choosing one option over others.

Integrity is essentially your personal moral compass.

Being clear about who you are and what you stand for—your personal integrity—is a good place to start.

When you are at a crossroads and are not sure which path to take, especially when all paths seem equally good and acceptable, the strength of your personal character is what helps you. Equally important is the reality that once you choose a path you will find it easy to live with your decision, however difficult it might have been to have chosen that path. It is this power that will help you manage the stress that can arise due to the trade-off that had to be made.

Integrity Cannot Be Mandated

The best example that I have seen of integrity in action—'what you do when no one is watching'—is among the Japanese. In the 1980s, when foreign travel was very limited and expensive, foreign travel by Indians was largely to the UAE and to Singapore. Those days it was very common to see people returning from these two countries walking out of the airport with two cartons in their hands—one a popular brand of video cassette recorder (VCR) and the other a two-in-one radio-and-audio-cassette player. People returning from Singapore would talk about the amazing level of discipline, order and cleanliness that one could see in that country. Singapore was in many ways the gold standard for Indians. In those days not many people from India travelled to Japan. The country was just coming into its own and taking over the world in areas ranging from consumer electronics to automobiles. Sony and Toyota were becoming the new household names in the Western world.

In 1985, on my first trip abroad as an adult, I went to both Japan and Singapore on the same trip. I visited Japan before going to Singapore. The short stay in Japan was an eye-opener and a lesson I have not forgotten even after thirty-five years. The level of personal discipline displayed by every Japanese was remarkable.

I did not know it then, but I got an early lesson in integrity from the Japanese.

I remember my colleagues and I walking down a deserted street around 10.30 p.m. in a small town, Hammamatsu, which houses the headquarters of Suzuki Motor Company. As we came to a traffic light, we saw a middle-aged person waiting for the pedestrian green light to cross the road. There was no vehicle in sight for a kilometre in any direction. Yet this man waited patiently for the light to change from red to green to cross the road. As I think of this incident over the years, I realize there cannot be a better example of integrity—what you do when no one is watching. As we spent a few days in Japan, I saw that the man in Hammamatsu was not an exception in that country. This was the norm. This feature could be seen in almost all aspects of Japanese actions and behaviour.

The visit to Singapore was good, but in many ways, it did not have the excitement we were told about since I had visited Japan first. The discipline, order and cleanliness in Singapore were definitely of a very high order. But when you compared them with what Japan had obtained, it was really nothing to write home about. I personally think Japan was on a different plane altogether. I saw one significant difference, however, between Japan and Singapore. In Japan one does not see any signs indicating punitive measures for breaking the law. Singapore is full of such signs. The question that struck me was—does discipline for these two countries come from within the citizens or from without? The answer was quite obvious.

For the Japanese, the drive to follow norms and rules seems to be something intrinsic to their culture. They do not seem to need the fear of fines and penalties. They do it even when 'no one is watching'! After a gap of almost twenty-eight years I visited Japan again in 2018. I saw that nothing much had changed in Japanese behaviour with respect to this aspect. They still stood at traffic lights despite no traffic on the road; there was not a piece of paper or litter in any part of the country that we visited over twelve days. Their civic sense and discipline came from within and they needed no watching over.

Contrast this with India. When I was younger it used to anger me, but now it saddens me to see the absolute disregard for rules and no respect for the law when people break traffic rules and parking restrictions. This, unfortunately, cuts across all cross sections of drivers—rich and poor, educated and illiterate, men and women, government and private. This happens not just in isolated places but in dense traffic areas and during peak hours too. I often feel awkward waiting for a green light at 5.30 a.m. when buses and cars go past me, oblivious to the red light. It calls for a lot of grit and commitment to control the urge to break the light. There are any number of examples we see around us every day—at no-parking areas, no-horn zones . . . A matter of concern in India is that even the so-called educated and socially aware are culpable in these matters. To make it worse, in many cases the lawmakers themselves are the lawbreakers. Government buses drive through red lights, indifferent to any norm or law; government cars are parked in no parking zones without a care. Do those responsible for this qualify as people with integrity?

What did I learn from the Japanese? Adherence to rules and the letter of the law can be mandated and imposed by the carrot-and-stick method to a large extent. Integrity cannot, however, be mandated. Integrity can be printed on mission and vision statements. That does not necessarily make people or organizations strong on integrity. Integrity has to be part of one's DNA. Our basic character. Integrity can only be shown through consistent action and not by talk.

Integrity—Brand You

Being a marketing person, I find that many situations in life have marketing analogies. In this case, personal integrity is essentially the brand promise. A good strong brand has focus and is very clear about what it stands for. The core of the brand is non-negotiable. Many strong brands have stood the test of time because of this clarity—think Nike, Apple, Maruti, Amul, Maggie; as much as numerous brands that have fallen by the wayside because of diluting their core proposition or trying to be too many things to too many people.

I will risk it to say that I am a die-hard Apple fan. So let me take this brand that has grown from strength to strength over the years. The integrity of the brand lies in some non-negotiable characteristics—simplicity, intuitive, perfection, premium. These characteristics are reflected in all aspects of Apple's operations, from product design and packaging to their website and even to the Apple stores. The three aspects of integrity come across clear in Apple:

- clarity on what I stand for
- others know what to expect of me
- I deliver consistently

It is this confidence and trust generated by Apple that commands premiums for their products and makes them the most valuable brand and most profitable company in the world.

Paradox—It Is Okay to Be Dishonest For but Not Dishonest With

I have observed paradoxical situations people are often faced with in organizations and as individuals. We see contradictions between what is acceptable in the organizational interest and the norms laid down for personal actions and behaviour.

As part of marketing and public relations initiatives, companies woo important clients by various means. A common and apparently acceptable method is to offer invitations to important events. For example, companies have their private boxes in major international sports events—the Olympics, World Cup events, Grand Slam tournaments, and the like. Or companies give away attractive goodies at high-end sponsored golf tournaments, like expensive golf bags, golfing equipment and accessories. Many corporate executives seem to have no qualms of conscience in accepting such invitations and gifts. I put a hypothetical question to my CEO friends. Instead of giving you an invitation or goodie, if the company instead gave you cash saying that this could be exchanged for the special box pass or the goodie in a nominated outlet, would they accept it? The answer is an immediate, unqualified no!

This leaves me wondering if there is a real difference between the two situations described above. In one case the conscience is clear because you are accepting a ticket or a goodie, while in the other case you feel 'dirty' because you are accepting cash, which is really to be traded in for the tickets. In my mind I am clear that there is absolutely no difference. In both cases there is a favour extended by one party to another. The manner of transaction is slightly different. More importantly, the company offering these incentives knows clearly why it is doing it—to influence, plain and simple. Yet one behaviour seems acceptable while the other is a definite no.

Now take another situation. The same executive who invites an important client to an event as described above does a minor fudge of a business expense report and is caught. What would be the outcome for this executive? The company code of ethics would be thrown at this person and he would be out of a job the next day.

Here comes the paradox. In both cases the executive was dishonest—inviting a client, which was a subtle way of influencing him, and fudging an expense report which was against the rules of the company. Yet the former is absolutely acceptable to the organization while the latter is not.

Let me share another interesting situation where executives bend rules to suit their convenience. At a leading IIM, there is a norm/practice/rule that at the time of final campus placements companies are not allowed to woo specific students before the formal interview process begins on campus. This, presumably, is to make it an even playing field for both the students and the potential recruiters, all of whom are important in the B-school system. Some companies work around this rule by asking alumni of a previous batch to identify potential students whom they would know and inviting them for a chat over a meal before the formal placement process starts.

Question 1: Is what the company doing dishonest?

Question 2: Is what the alumnus doing dishonest?

Question 3: Is what the student doing dishonest?

One does not need to be a great philosopher to know the answers. The organization (executive) knows that this is dishonest, the alumnus knows it is dishonest, and of course the student knows it is dishonest. Yet all of them are invariably willing parties to this subtle violation of a norm and conveniently turn a blind eye to it. The issues I discuss in my classes, and which we need to seriously think about, are:

- Why these people do what they do.
- How people are willing to bend rules to meet personal goals at the cost of personal integrity and social norms.
- How would you feel working for a boss who is inherently dishonest, asks you to be dishonest when he wants it that way and yet expects you to be honest otherwise?
- With what moral authority can your boss expect honesty from you or you from your team?
- Does the student have the courage of conviction to tell the interviewing company that they are breaking rules and that the student will be happy to attend the interview as per the institute's norms?

These are moments in one's life that define one's personality. These are questions that each of us has to answer for ourselves. This is where clarity in our personal value system is essential. No one else can help, since it is we who have to live with our decisions.

Here again, I discuss a reality paradox as in the earlier situation—it is acceptable to the boss for the subordinate to be dishonest *for* him but he will not tolerate dishonesty from the subordinate *with* him. Strange, isn't it?

The above examples lead me to my hypothesis that many organizations and individuals seem to have the following unwritten rule:

> It is alright to be dishonest for the company but
> It is not alright to be dishonest with the company.

Honesty and integrity are bent to suit one's convenience.

Some of My Defining Moments

I have often wondered what defines me and what situations or incidents might have given me some insight into myself as a person. As in all introspections or memoirs, it is easy to retrofit and conclude—QED. Like many people, I have always prided myself on my honesty and sense of integrity. This is a truism. No one would like to say that he/she is dishonest or lacks integrity. So I delved into my past to unearth some defining moments to confirm whether honesty and integrity were indeed my core characteristics or what I deluded myself into believing I had. I describe three incidents that I believe reaffirm a basic trait in me and reassures me that I do walk the talk when it comes to integrity. Interestingly, all three incidents relate to a period when I was just moving up the corporate ladder and the desire to move fast was high. In retrospect, I am glad that I did what I did and got clarity about myself as time went by.

1. The year was 1984. I was a young head of marketing at a new company introducing new-generation motorcycles. As part of my job I had to appoint a national network of dealers and finalize contracts with transporters for moving our motorcycles to different parts of the country. One young transporter from Delhi would keep following up with me for a transport contract, and I would keep telling him that he would get the contract when we finalized all others. On each visit he would invite me to dinner and I would decline. One time, in a weak moment, maybe because he was about my age and seemed a nice guy, I told him I would have one drink with him on his next visit. So we had that one drink at his hotel the next time. Afterwards, as I was leaving the hotel, he put his hand in his pocket and pulled

out a thick envelope. I was taken aback, knowing what it was. I asked him, 'What is this?' His reply, which is fresh in my mind even after thirty-six years, was, '*Rakho*, sir. *Kaam ayega*!' (Keep it, sir. It will come in handy.) I told him that I did not know what my response should be—to laugh, cry, get angry or feel sad. He tried convincing me to take the envelope and also realized that he had made an error in doing what he did. I finally closed the discussion with the statement—'You know why I cannot take the envelope? Because when you walk into my office tomorrow morning, I will look you in the eye and throw you out of my office. That pleasure will be taken away from me.'

2. Around the same time, I also had the responsibility of appointing dealers for our company. The demand for dealerships was very high. Our product was the first of the new-generation motorcycles in the country, and dealers would do good business with our products. A colleague mentioned to me that one rejected dealer-applicant was sending out a story that he did not get the dealership because another party had bought me out. I was shocked and angry. My boss, an industry veteran, told me not to take it personally since such stories were par for the course in my kind of job. Being young, hot-blooded and inexperienced in this kind of a role, it rankled me. Finally, I went to my managing director with an undated resignation letter and told him the story. He smiled and asked me to forget about it. I told him to keep my letter, saying, 'You can question my competence, capability and skills, but the day you question my integrity, put the date on the letter and tell me. Integrity is the only real asset I have and I will neither have it doubted nor put up a defence for it.'
3. Another small incident links with my discovery of the core. In the same organization, I moved from head of marketing to head of purchase. At that time there was a vendor whom I knew well before I took on the purchase role. One Diwali he

came home and brought a sari saying it was for '*bhabhiji*'. I refused to take it. He insisted, saying that it was a gesture, as part of his friendship of years and not the business relationship we now had. On my next visit to Delhi, I made a point of going to his home to meet the family and gave '*bhabhiji*' a sari. That was the last time he ever made a move to give me anything, even though our relationship as friends continued. And I could sleep easy.

As I think back and look at various incidents and interactions in my life, I am clear that having my honesty beyond question has been a very important part of my personality. I see in my transactions and experiences with people that I have valued being honest and open as a defining characteristic. I rarely shy away from telling people how I see a situation or action, as much as I value people being honest with me rather than trying to sugar-coat an unpalatable feedback. In this process I find that we know exactly where we stand with respect to another person and hence can plan and prepare appropriately. Being honest and open is not to be confused with having a licence to hurt or belittle others and cheat the system. The important thing is that this honesty stems from being true to one's conscience.

What does this do for you? It allows you to hold your head high and look a person in the eye at all times. One is confident of one's actions and behaviour and also knows where it comes from. It does have its downsides too. You can be seen as arrogant, obstinate, inflexible and so on. Remember it is all about trade-offs, the ability to live with yourself and, importantly, about sleeping well.

The Power of Integrity

A Man for All Seasons is a classic 1966 Hollywood film which won six Academy awards, including for the best picture, best director and best actor. The film revolves around two characters, the British king Henry VIII and his chancellor, Sir Thomas More. Students of history might know that Henry VIII was known for his six marriages. As a monarch he wanted to break away from the Catholic church so as to annul his first marriage as he could not get an heir to the throne from his wife. Henry VIII was very close to More and valued his friendship and counsel. The film revolves round More, who is portrayed as the ultimate man of conscience, and who remains true to his principles and religion under all circumstances and at all times. He did not accede to the king's demand that he approve the annulment of his marriage and go against the Pope, even though all others in the court of Henry VIII approved the disengagement of Britain from the Catholic Church. The fact that all of England was willing to side with the King against the Pope was not good enough. Thomas More's approval of his actions was far more important to King Henry than that of the rest of England put together. In his anger, he trumped up charges of treason against More. It was clear that More would be sentenced to death for not siding with the King. In a very poignant scene towards the end of the film, More's daughter pleads with her father to sign the document approving the annulment of the king's marriage to his first wife so that More's life would be spared. He refuses, with these last words to his daughter:

> When a man takes an oath he's holding himself in his hands like water
> If he opens his fingers then, he need not hope to find himself again.

Why is this story relevant? Interestingly, when I went to head The Lawrence School in Ooty in 2005, I felt an urge to watch this film, which I remembered I had seen in my college days. What I did not realize was the impact this film had made on me. It was only upon seeing it again in 2005 that it occurred to me that I had first seen this film as a sixteen-year-old, and that thirty-seven years later it still made a strong impression on me. This film became a part of the curriculum for my students in the school, and subsequently in the college I headed, for our discussion on the role of values and principles in one's life. Interestingly, when I asked students which scene in the film made the most impact on them, a large majority would mention the above-quoted dialogue between the daughter and father.

Another strong message from the film is relevant for all of us at all times. Thomas More's actions drive home the point about the amount of respect and value given to people who show strong character in terms of integrity and principles. What mattered to Henry VIII was not what the whole of England did but what Thomas More thought.

> People who display high levels of integrity may not always be liked but will always be respected.

I could probably relate to Thomas More because of my grandfather, fondly called 'KSV *mama*' by most of his family and friends, who was a role model for many of us in the family. A story that we often heard from him stuck with all his grandchildren. He was one of the early Indian engineering graduates in the country. In 1947, at the time of Independence, he was the senior-most Indian in a British engineering company. The company would not make him the CEO because he was Indian. They promised to give him all terms and conditions of employment as given to an Englishman who would be the head of the company. On principle, my grandfather resigned.

He was just fifty years old at that time. He settled down in his hometown in Tamil Nadu. As family, we only knew him as a man with three dhotis, four cotton shirts, two pairs of slippers, a walking stick and an umbrella. He gave up all the perks and luxuries of a good job because of his principles. Interestingly, not once did we grandkids hear a word of regret or remorse about the action he took at the prime of his career. He knew where his compass directed him. He made his trade-off and slept peacefully.

Integrity—Intent Versus Execution: Easier Said Than Done

Almost all vision, mission or core values statements of organizations will carry the word 'integrity' or its equivalents, such as 'honesty', 'trustworthiness', 'commitment' or 'principles'. Putting them in statements is the easy part. Living them is the difficult part. In the race for success, revenues, profits, market share, shareholder value and market capitalization, managements are willing to turn a blind eye to many undesirable activities. Even worse, they seem willing to get into doing things that are not only unethical but illegal. In the process, they let down all the stakeholders of the company. We have seen a few cases in the earlier chapter.

Let us take a relook at three companies that were mentioned earlier, in Chapter 5. Three organizations with different backgrounds, leaders in their own right, had one thing in common: they cheated their stakeholders. There is a big disconnect between what they said in their vision statements and what they did in practice.

Enron Corporation[2]

This is probably the most famous of all corporate scandals, and we could say the forerunner for many others that have followed in this century. Enron was a Houston, Texas-based American energy, commodities and services company. In the year 2000, Enron had claimed revenues of nearly $101 billion for the year. *Fortune* named Enron 'America's Most Innovative Company' for six consecutive years. The company went bankrupt in 2001.

In 2001, it was revealed that Enron's reported financial condition was sustained by institutionalized, systematic and creatively planned accounting fraud. Enron is now a well-known example of wilful corporate fraud and corruption. In Enron's accounting fraud scandal, shareholders lost US$74 billion; thousands of employees and investors lost their retirement accounts; and of course many employees lost their jobs. Interestingly, the scandal also took with it Arthur Andersen, which had been Enron's main auditor for years. Arthur Andersen was one of the five largest accounting firms in the United States at the time, with a reputation for high standards and quality risk management.

Ironically, Enron's values statement included:

> INTEGRITY
> We work with customers and prospects openly, honestly, and sincerely. When we say we will do something, we will do it; when we say we cannot or will not do something, then we won't do it.

Wells Fargo[3]

Wells Fargo, America's fourth-largest bank in its time, perpetrated a fraud involving fake accounts and cross-selling by employees under pressure to meet sales quotas. According to the Justice Department, the fraudulent operation was carried out by thousands of Wells Fargo employees over a period of more than ten years. The bank paid a $3-billion fine to settle a civil lawsuit. The fraud also claimed the heads of many senior executives, including that of the bank's chairman and CEO John Stumpf, who had been with the bank for thirty-two years.

A look at the bank's 'vision, values and goals' throws up the following:

'Our five values, which articulate what's most important to us: What's right for customers, people as a competitive advantage, ethics, diversity and inclusion, and leadership.'

Volkswagen[4]

I am sure you need no introduction to Volkswagen. It is amongst the two top automakers in the world. In 2015, the Environmental Protection Agency (EPA) of USA found that many VW cars being sold in America had a software designed to cheat the testing process. This was commonly called a 'defeat device'. The software could detect when the vehicles were being tested and changed their performance accordingly to improve results. The results showed that cars would in some cases exceed nitrogen oxide norms by up to forty times the permissible limits. Volkswagen confessed to manipulating eleven million vehicles worldwide to fool emission tests by installing the cheating software in them. With a huge number of lawsuits against the company, Volkswagen has paid over $30 billion in fines and is still counting. Two former Volkswagen executives are serving prison terms in the United States for their role in trying to cover up the emissions fraud. Martin Winterkorn, Volkswagen's former chief executive, faces criminal charges in the United States and Germany for his alleged role in the scheme.

A look at Volkswagen's vision and mission statements tell us that its core values comprise 'accountability, teamwork, servant's attitude, and integrity. We want Volkswagen to be a company with integrity through and through and to be respected in the best sense of the word.'

The examples above are not exceptions. In the last few years, we have heard of scams, scandals and frauds in the world of business almost on a daily basis. The corporate world is a graveyard of organizations that have not been able to translate intent to action when it comes to integrity. These scams are not innocuous, random, isolated incidents that might have been overlooked by internal management or the external auditors or regulators. They are perpetrated consciously by senior management and extend over years. Such incidents are also not limited to small-time companies or people but involve giant multinational corporations and involve cheating of unthinkable magnitude. I have chosen just three from among the numerous frauds and scandals that have happened. I have chosen these three because they are from different industries, environments and time periods. And they are huge organizations. We also find that in almost all such cases of fraud, companies have knowingly and willingly flouted rules and broken laws over years, which could only have been done with the knowledge and connivance of senior management. A simple search on the internet for corporate scams/scandals will give you a large number of hits.

What has corporate fraud got to with this book and personal integrity? The simple reality is that organizational integrity starts with personal integrity. Organizations, groups and teams are only collections of people. The value system of an organization can only be a reflection of the collective values of the people that run them. We are all part of a social system in all aspects of our lives. We are part of various groups, be they in the family, at work, on the sports field, in our social lives, and so on. We thus have the possibilities of both moulding the values of our individual ecosystems and getting influenced by the value systems of these ecosystems. In the process, as we have seen earlier, there will be dilemmas when there is conflict between the value systems of the self and the group. It is for these times that clarity about one's own personal value system and one's integrity levels come of help.

To Sum Up

Today the market is flooded with biographies and memoirs of people. Of course, all these people would be successful in their chosen fields, or else who would be interested in their stories. Many of these stories are documented as though all of life was well charted and laid out for them and they knew who they were and what they were capable of achieving. Rarely does it happen like this in real life. As in management books and case studies, we see something happening in real life and try to fit the results into a framework. This retrofitting is just a perspective of the author. It is easy to give lessons in hindsight. The challenge for us is to acquire foresight—know where one is going and how to get there so that the chances of reaching our destination are higher. The purpose is also to make the journey as enjoyable and fun as possible so that we can look forward to the journey rather than see it as a drag. One characteristic that helps in this process is integrity.

The importance of integrity was well summed up by Warren Buffet.

> Look for three things in a person—intelligence, energy and integrity. If they don't have the last one, don't even bother with the first two.

In this journey, as in any travel, we will face roadblocks, barriers, or come to a crossroads or a fork with no clear road sign as to where the paths lead. We will have to make choices and trade-offs. At times like these, the core of your personality—what you are, what you want and what you will do to get what you want—will be very important for the navigation. There is no guarantee that one path is better than another, but the journey will certainly be better with this clarity. I will amplify on this as we conclude this book.

My learnings on integrity can be summed up in these four remarks:

- Dishonesty is not the same as cheating. There is a difference between the letter of law and the spirit of it.
- Integrity cannot be mandated—it has to be an integral part of one's character.
- Personal integrity/character is the main asset of an individual, which cannot be taken away by anyone. Lose that and you have lost everything.
- Integrity can only be taught by living it.

We have to remember that there are no absolutes when it comes to principles and integrity. Each of us has to decide our own boundaries, negotiables and non-negotiables, and that will be our moral compass. This compass will give us the strength to take tough decisions and live with them without regret. You can be a Vishy, Gilly or Roddick, or equally be a Maradona. And this is not to say that one is better than the other as a person.

Mahatma Gandhi said:

> Happiness is when what you think, what you say and what you do are in harmony.

Decide who you are or want to be and live it accordingly. That's it.

7

INTERACT: PEOPLE MATTER

Robin Williams: Hollywood actor widely regarded by critics as one of the funniest comedians of all time. Winner of numerous awards, including an Oscar for best supporting actor, six Golden Globe awards and four Grammy's. In August 2014, Williams hanged himself. He was sixty-three years old.

Marilyn Monroe: American actress, model and singer. She became one of the most popular sex symbols of the 1950s and early 1960s. She died from an overdose of barbiturates, with her death being ruled a probable suicide. She was thirty-six at the time of her death.

Ernest Hemingway: Winner of the 1954 Nobel Prize in Literature. Died by suicide at sixty-two.

V.G. Siddhartha: Indian businessman, founder, chairman and managing director of the Café Coffee Day chain. He was reputed to have the largest holding of coffee plantations in India. He killed himself by jumping into a river in 2019. He was aged sixty.

Vineet Whig: Chief operating officer of Encyclopaedia Britannica. Committed suicide by jumping down a deep shaft of his apartment building in Gurugram. He was forty-seven.

The people mentioned above have three things in common:

1. They were all reasonably wealthy.
2. They were most definitely successful people in their chosen fields of work.
3. They all ended their lives prematurely, probably in the prime of their careers.

Money can't buy happiness; people can help get you happiness.

Each one of the persons mentioned above had every reason to be happy and to want to live life to the fullest. They are unfortunately not just random exceptions. If money and success could buy happiness it would be wonderful for many people. No rich or successful person would be unhappy and, more importantly, none of them would take the extreme step of committing self-harm and suicide. Yet, we have seen in the earlier chapter that suicides are in fact on the rise, despite all measures of wealth showing improvement over the years. There are many reasons why people go to the extreme step of taking their lives. It is not in the scope of this book to discuss them. The only one thing I can say with certainty is that these people were not happy with their lives. What I do know is that no one who is happy thinks of taking the extreme step they did.

What can money do? Money can certainly buy physical and material comforts. You can get larger houses, nicer cars, comfortable beds, cooler rooms, hassle-free travel, international holidays, fetch your friends' and neighbours' envy, and what have you. Remember pleasure? The hedonic treadmill? Yes, it can get you all of that. But, obviously, it cannot buy happiness.

This brings me to the second I for happiness—**Interact**.

Happiness is no doubt a state that is driven internally by an individual. However, I have learnt through experience that the people around you can significantly aid you in the process of making you happy or unhappy. At a basic level, this is not difficult to understand. Think back to times and days when you were truly happy. Was it when you were alone or when you were with people? Think back over the years to the kind of people you have been happiest with, and you will get most of your answers. Happiness is about building and sustaining healthy relationships.

Interactions are about relationships. Relationship can be described as the way we are connected with someone. In this chapter we will explore the importance of people and our interactions with them to achieve our goal of happiness.

The Changed World, Relationships and the Social System

'Man is a social animal' is an old saying. The famous psychologist Abraham Maslow's hierarchy of needs is a good place to start to understand the importance of relationships for us humans. Maslow's motivational theory in psychology comprises a five-tier model of human needs, often depicted as levels within a pyramid.[1]

According to Maslow, people go up the pyramid after satisfying their lower-level needs. At the base are man's physiological needs—the basic human needs of *roti*, *kapda*, *makaan* (food, clothing and shelter). The next level is what he calls safety needs—we need to feel safe and secure. Once these basic needs are satisfied, the next requirements are psychological needs. The first of these is the need for belonging. This encompasses intimate relationships and love. He then moves up the pyramid to the need for self-esteem, and finally at the top of the pyramid is the need for self-actualization.

The important and interesting point to note in Maslow's pyramid is that after we satisfy our basic physical needs, we actually have a need to belong. This could imply belonging in any context—personal, family, social or professional. The need to belong brings to light the importance of relationships. That is what makes the quality of our relationships so important—to ensure and reinforce a sense of belonging, and thus our overall well-being. We have talked about the changing world and its impact on the individual and her happiness. We will now look at the world today and its impact on and implications for relationships and, consequently, our happiness.

There is a huge difference in the world in which your grandparents brought up your parents and the one in which you have been brought up by your parents. The changes have not only been in the area of technology and material comforts but also in the social fabric of our lives. A lot of it has definitely been for the better. There are some areas where things have not been so good for the current generation of people between the ages of twenty-five and forty, and this is where you, dear reader, have to be watchful.

The changes in one's way of life resulting from development, industrialization and progress have had a major impact on the quality and quantity of social interactions and relationships. India has thrived on the concept of joint and extended families. Various generations of people in a family would live under the same roof, and this formed a tremendous support system for people. No one ever grew up or lived alone. There was always someone to play with, talk to and help out when needed. If anything, getting time to oneself might have been the challenge in the olden days! With improving communication and travel, opportunities for study and work have extended far beyond the immediacy of one's town, district, state or even country. This change in the ecosystem has resulted in a significant change in the social fabric of our society. The traditional joint-family system has given way to smaller, nuclear families. We often find ourselves far from our near and dear ones, and either distance or other preoccupations prevent us from being with each other often enough.

What has this to do with our happiness and well-being?

In 2002, two pioneers of 'positive psychology', Ed Diener and Martin Seligman, conducted a study at the University of Illinois on the 10 per cent of students with the highest scores recorded on a survey of personal happiness. They found that the most salient characteristics shared by students who were very happy and showed the fewest signs of depression were 'their strong ties to friends and family and commitment to spending time with them'.[2]

Harvard University has what is considered one of the world's longest studies of adult life. Harvard Study of Adult Development, which started in 1938, continues till date. The study, which tracks the lives of 724 men over the years, is now in the second phase of tracking the lives of the next generation of these men. In a popular Ted Talk in 2015, Robert Waldinger, a psychiatrist and a professor at Harvard Medical School and the director of the study, disclosed some interesting findings from the study. He summed up three lessons on relationships from this study.[3,4]

1. ***Social connections are really good for us, and loneliness kills.*** People who are more socially connected to family, friends and community are happier; they are physically healthier and they live longer than people who are less well connected. On the contrary, keeping to yourself and experiencing loneliness is toxic. People who are more isolated than they want to be from others find that they are less happy; their health declines earlier in midlife, their brain functioning declines sooner, and they live shorter lives than people who are not lonely.
2. ***When it comes to relationships, pick quality over quantity.*** Waldinger said that when it comes to friends, it's not about the number of friends you have, but 'it's the quality of your close relationships that matters'.

3. ***Good relationships protect your brain.***
   Waldinger explained that in addition to positively affecting your physical and emotional health, good relationships have the power to sharpen your memory. 'Taking care of your body is important, but tending to your relationships is a form of self-care too. That, I think, is the revelation.'

Relationships and Loneliness: Flip Sides of a Coin

This brings us to the flip side of having meaningful relationships—loneliness. It is extremely paradoxical that we are living in a world which has never been connected as much as it is today. We have the internet, smartphones, 5G speeds, huge bandwidths, sophisticated yet simple-to-use software and apps. With significant developments in travel and transportation and the general improvement in the well-being of people, there is no part of the world that cannot be accessed literally at the click of a button.

For a person like me who grew up in the just-after-Independence era with rationing, shortages and no options in whatever we wanted to buy, the India of 2021 is a completely different country. The world today is connected both physically and virtually. Higher incomes and affordable travel have made national and international travel almost an impulse activity for many. I often think back to my early years in the late 1970s. My father was one of the first Indians to officiate as an umpire at Wimbledon. For five years he would go to Wimbledon. As an umpire he would get passes for the tournament, including for some major matches in the centre court. We are a tennis-loving family, and obviously Wimbledon, the Mecca of tennis, is a dream for any tennis lover. Yet I know that in all the years that he went to Wimbledon, it did not even occur to me that I could fulfil a Wimbledon dream, and that too in style.

England was a far-off land which only a lucky few could visit. My dream was finally realized about twenty-five years later!

Today I see youngsters travelling to different parts of the world, literally 'for kicks'. A pre-wedding stag or a bachelorette blast in Romania. A girls'-only bash in Bali or Egypt. A theme wedding in Phuket. These are very common amongst middle-class youngsters of today. This is of course not counting the get-togethers within the country. No place is too far.

What am I leading to? We are living in a highly connected world of 24/7/365 messaging, texting, video calling and travelling. We have the ubiquitous social media, which is an integral part of one's life, from wake-up to sleep time, and often in the middle of the night too. With these levels of connectivity, one would think that the strength of our relationships would be high and the bonds between people strong. Ironically, the reverse seems to be true. We are getting more disconnected in a highly connected world. Let's see the implications of this paradox.

Loneliness: A Cause for Concern

According to a study of loneliness—reportedly the largest ever—done by the BBC with 55,000 participants in 2018, 33 per cent of respondents reported they 'often', or 'very often' feel lonely. More interesting and of concern is that the highest concentration of 40 per cent of these respondents is among those aged sixteen to twenty-four.[5] Despite high levels of connectivity, studies and trends seem to indicate that we are in fact getting lonelier and more socially disconnected.

According to a 2018 survey by the *Economist* and the Kaiser Family Foundation (KFF), more than two in ten adults in the United States (22 per cent) and the United Kingdom (23 per cent) say they always or often feel lonely, lack companionship, or feel left out or isolated. Loneliness isn't just an American phenomenon. In Japan, there are more than half a million people under forty who haven't left their houses or interacted with anyone for at least six months. In Canada, the share of solo households is 28 per cent; across the European Union it is 34 per cent. Loneliness is very much around.[6]

A 2016 Viceland UK Census reported that loneliness is the number one fear among young people today—ranking ahead of losing one's home or job. Fully 42 per cent of millennial women are more afraid of loneliness than a cancer diagnosis, by far the highest share of any generation. This fear has been ingrained into the very lexicon of millennials, immortalized in acronyms like FOMO (fear of missing out).[6] US Census Bureau researches shows that a hundred years ago, fewer than 6 per cent of all households consisted of people who lived alone. By 2013 it stood at 28 per cent.[7]

Loneliness: Why Should it Matter?

Studies point to findings that loneliness not only affects people's physical and mental health but also has an impact on mortality. A 2010 research published by psychology professor Julianne Holt-Lunstad showed that being disconnected posed a danger comparable to smoking fifteen cigarettes a day and was more predictive of early death than the effects of air pollution or physical inactivity. Another meta-analysis examined the impact that social isolation, loneliness or living alone might have on mortality. Researchers found that all three had a significant and equal effect on the risk of premature death.[8]

I need to make a quick distinction between loneliness and being alone. It is not just a matter of semantics. Feeling lonely is about a sense of isolation in a person, the feeling that something is missing. It has negative connotations. Being alone, on the other hand, is about solitude. It is about enjoying one's own company and being at peace with oneself. You can be alone but not lonely and you can be with people and yet be lonely.

As I write this chapter, the world lost one young and successful person. Tony Hsieh promoted an online shoe delivery company called Zappos. He was bought over by Amazon for $1.2 billion. He died in a house fire in November 2020. According to a report in *Forbes* magazine, Hsieh's high-profile lifestyle had spiralled as he battled mental health issues and drug addiction.[9,10] Ironically, in his autobiography *Delivering Happiness: A Path to Profits, Passion and Purpose,* Hsieh expounded his belief that happiness is achieved by focusing on spreading joy among friends, employees and customers. What one gathers from reports is that Tony Hsieh was not happy. Forbes also says, 'He fostered so much human connection and happiness, yet there was this void. It was difficult for him to be alone.' Tony Hsieh was forty-six years old and worth an estimated $800 million at the time of his death. Money could not buy him happiness.

From what we have seen so far, it is safe to say that loneliness is dangerous and harmful.

Social Media—Boon or Bane?

This brings us to the great connector—social media. Products like Facebook, WhatsApp, Skype, Twitter, Instagram and Zoom are some of the best things that have happened to us in recent years. They are meant to improve connections between people. Hence the term social media. The question is, have they really helped in bringing people closer or have they ended up distancing people in a real sense. While these are amazing innovations, let us examine their role in making us happy. Or unhappy.

What we see is that despite the tremendous benefits that social media offers in terms of connecting with people, everything is really not so hunky-dory. This is a matter that Gen X and Gen Y need to look at seriously, because the internet, smartphone and social media are something they have grown up with and are an intrinsic part of their lives. They are taken for granted. The long-term impact of these technologies is not necessarily factored in. Researchers are also slowly coming to grips with it, with a lot of interesting findings on their effects and impact. I am sure you are aware of a lot that is written about the benefits, dangers and pitfalls of social media. I will hence limit my thoughts to some of their effects in the context of our goal—happiness.

Smartphones were introduced in 2007. By 2015, 92 per cent of teens and young adults in the US owned a smartphone. In a 2017 study of over half a million students from eighth through twelfth grades, it was found that the number exhibiting high levels of depressive symptoms increased by 33 per cent between 2010 and 2015. The rise in depressive symptoms correlates with smartphone adoption during that period, even when matched year by year, observes the study's lead author psychologist Jean Twenge of San Diego State University. She also found that compared with the late 1980s, high school seniors heading to college in 2016 spent an 'hour less a day engaging in in-person social interaction', such as going to parties, movies or on car rides with friends. This decline was associated with increased digital media use by the students as a group. The study also found that adolescents who spent the most time on social media and the least time in face-to-face social interactions reported the most loneliness.[11]

Over that same period there was a sharp increase of 30 per cent in students seeking help at college and university counselling centres, principally for depression and anxiety.[12]

These numbers are very telling and need to be looked at seriously. One big difference between the lives of today's teenagers and young adults and the earlier generations is that they spend much less time connecting with their peers in person. Connections are more electronic and through social media. 'The less you are connected with human beings in a deep, empathic way, the less you're really getting the benefits of a social interaction,' points out Alexandra Hamlet, PsyD, a clinical psychologist at the Child Mind Institute, New York.[13]

Social Media: A Great Way to Connect and Divide

Social media has changed the way we meet and interact with each other. The positive aspects of social media need little or no discussion. It has provided people with methods of locating other people, staying in touch with them and continuing interactions with them on a regular basis. This is especially so for families that are separated from each other by long distances and cannot meet as often as they would like to. One group of beneficiaries are grandparents, who can now connect with their grandchildren regularly before the kids grow up and have little time for them. I find that grandparents treasure these moments. It's also great for partners, spouses and children who have to stay away from their families, for whatever reason. Video calls and regular chats reduce the pain of separation.

Any tool, technology or equipment is only as good as we make it. As much as developments have significant positive impacts, we also see that they have their share of side effects. Let us look at some of the not-so-desirable impacts of social media. Studies show that increased usage of social media, amongst other factors, may lead to issues of self-esteem and conflict in relationships.

FOMO. You can get trapped in the fear-of-missing-out (FOMO) syndrome. On your Facebook or Instagram page you find some happening in your group to which you were not invited. This takes you by surprise. This can be quite a source of stress, especially for younger people. You feel left out. As we know from Maslow, the need to belong is high, and not being invited to a group event when you expected to can be seen as rejection by your peer group.

Envy. I have spoken at length about envy in the earlier chapter. Social media can only add to the triggers that will set us envying others since it exposes us to so many events and happenings in the lives of people all over. The comparison factor in social media leads to envy. Studies show that social media use triggers feelings of envy across various cross-sections of people.[14,15] The social media platforms then become breeding grounds for invidious feelings and resentment. It can become a vicious cycle: envy can make a person want to make his or her own life look better and post envy-inducing posts of their own, pitching them into an endless vicious cycle of one-upping and feeling envious. This is not a healthy situation, especially amongst young people who are more vulnerable to negative emotions.[16]

Validation. I believe this is a matter that needs to be considered seriously. The number of likes on your Facebook page is an indication of the number of people who are reading you. We need to belong. One way of knowing we belong is to be acknowledged. That your friends are doing something without your knowledge gives you the message of being ignored or being kept out. We do not like it. The 'likes' show us we belong and give us a sense of comfort that our friends are still around. Another practice, which in my opinion should be a matter of concern, is the posting of very personal remarks and expression of personal emotions and feelings by people on social media, for reasons that I have still not fathomed. I see posts where people are talking about their partners, spouses and children in glowing terms on special occasions, such as anniversaries or birthdays.

'You are the best thing that has happened to me in my life . . .'

'I remember the day we first met . . .'

'You have brought such a sense of joy in my life . . .'

'Look forward to many more years of togetherness . . .'

These are very personal comments. I am still to figure out why a person cannot or will not say these things directly to the person whom they are addressing. Why should such matters be put on social media? The amateur psychologist in me says that they do this to get 'likes' and responses from their friends, such as:

'Oh, What a lovely thought, how beautiful.'

'You both are truly a made-in-heaven pair.'

'You are so blessed to have parents/a partner/children like this.'

These are the ego massages and feel-good connects we seem to be seeking. Ask yourself—honestly, how you would feel if you posted personal messages but got no responses such as the ones above on Facebook? Or if you got no WhatsApp messages from your close friends for a few days or even hours, and you know that these friends were in touch with each other? Are we seeking validation from our peers and friends on a regular basis? Do we constantly need external stimuli for us to feel good? We need to ask ourselves how strong our self-esteem and sense of self-worth are. That validation can only come from you.

Relationships: Infidelity, Suspicion, Jealousy, Separation

The changing landscape and the dynamics between men and women is well documented and much talked about, so I will spare you the details. What we are seeing quite definitely is the rampage of social media on relationships. Relationships between friends, colleagues, partners and family are often under pressure. I will talk a bit about the pressure on marital relationships, since this often has an impact that goes beyond just the two people in the relationship.

In my work as a volunteer-lay counsellor for about thirty years, I have seen a significant change in the dynamics of relationships of all kinds—marriage, family, professional and social. In many of today's relationships, both partners are often independent, strong-willed, self-assured people, and there is no obvious need for anyone to be submissive to the other. This tends to reduce the ability and patience for understanding and adjustment in relationships. Exit options are available for the partners and are often exercised by one or both. This is confirmed in the growing number of divorces and broken marriages over the years. One needs to be a strong, self-confident person to manage the challenges and demands of marital/romantic relationships.

One trend that has a big impact in the larger social context is that of divorce and separation in marriages and romantic relationships. Even though India has one of the lowest rates of divorce in the world, at 1 per cent, things are changing. According to a report from the Organisation for Economic Co-operation and Development, the absolute number of divorces in India has gone up from 1 in 1,000 to 13 in 1,000 over the last decade or so. This is significant. This is not counting the number of separations and break-ups of relationships outside of marriage.[17]

Social media provides easy access to information, not just about the present but about the past too. Very often information gets to us even if we are not seeking it. The social media platforms ensure it. Information about past relationships, innocuous pictures of current activities and movements can lead to unease in relationships. This can result in suspicion, which could border on paranoia, leading to increased monitoring of activities by one or the other partner, lack of trust and consequent deterioration of the relationship.

Tinder is an online dating application. Interestingly, 30 per cent of Tinder users are married. A site like Ashley Madison actually states: 'Life is short. Have an affair.' Also found on the website is the statement: 'Originally designed specifically for married men and women looking to have extramarital affairs in the most discreet way possible!' The company has a reported membership of 60 million people from fifty-three countries. The world has certainly changed.[18]

The proliferation of smartphones and the ever-innovative development of social media apps have made it extremely simple for people dissatisfied in a relationship to look out for new ones. One in three divorces now start as online affairs. As much as 8 per cent of adults in relationships admit to having secret social media accounts.[19]

A 2010 survey by the American Academy of Matrimonial Lawyers (AAML) found that four out of five lawyers used evidence derived from social networking sites in divorce cases, with Facebook leading the pack. It is also estimated that 30 per cent to 40 per cent of divorces happen because of social media-related issues, as outlined above.[20,21]

Adding to all of the above is the hard reality that in today's world of social media there is no real way of erasing your past. There is no way to destroy old letters, photographs, or move to another location to leave your past behind. Your life is stored in cyberspace and never truly leaves you. Your past can pop up anytime, anywhere. And not always to your advantage.

Final Thoughts

The long and short of what I have tried to convey is that people and relationships are important for happiness. We have seen that despite the phenomenal advances in connectivity and access, data seem to indicate that the strength of relationships is not necessarily going in a positive direction. I have learnt that we cannot take people and relationships for granted. We need make conscious efforts to build, nurture and sustain good relationships for our overall well-being and happiness. At the end of the day, we need to harness the power of technology and social media for our benefit and watch out for the downsides. Virtual connect does not have the same impact and effect as quality personal time with close friends and people who matter. In this chapter, I hope I have been able to highlight the importance of people and good relationships for our overall well being.

There are enough books, articles and talks on building and managing relationships. I am going to share the few things I have learnt, and which I practise, as my way of getting the best out of relationships. A lot of these are just common sense and intuitive understandings, and really do not need any great insight; you do not need to be a philosopher, sociologist or psychologist. It just needs a conviction that people matter. And a little sensitivity towards others.

Let's look at what are some of the basic things people look for when dealing with other people. Using Maslow's pyramid as a framework, after fulfilling our basic physiological and security needs, we have psychological needs. I have learnt that some of the psychological needs all human beings have, whether old or young, man or woman, rich or poor, literate or not, are:

- To feel respected
- To feel wanted
- To feel comfortable
- To feel important
- To feel understood
- To feel welcome
- To feel valued

As I look at the above needs, I realize that all I need to do to meet the them is to reinforce the personal touch. When you offer the personal touch to people, you in fact satisfy all or most of the above needs. Let me share with you a few of my favourite things that I have consciously practised over the years, which have helped me strengthen my connect with people.

Listen: This is the first and most important skill for building relationships. Any book on communication will tell you how to improve your listening skills. The question is, why should we be good listeners? For me the answer is simple—a good listener satisfies almost every need outlined above and hence listening is a very powerful tool with which to build bridges with people.

Be personal: I have been constantly amazed by the sense of impersonality, almost bordering on indifference, exhibited by people even of my generation in relationships, including those with close friends. This impersonality has been aggravated, thanks to mobile phones and to social media. I have never understood how one can send a greeting or condolence to email or WhatsApp groups. Adding to that, to make it quick, messages are even abbreviated. How can you send a friend a message like this one:

- HBD ☺, which I presume means happy birthday!

Even worse is to send impersonal condolences on group mails and messages. Common among them are:

- RIP
- Om Shanti
- I pray for the departed soul. (This one always intrigues me. One must be spending a major part of the day praying for departed people! I am also sure most people have done quite well in their lives without our prayers and their being in our thoughts. In my view, such comments do not communicate honesty and genuineness.)

Responses have become so standard and mechanical that it takes away from the essence of what one should be doing to strengthen a relationship. The amateur psychologist in me tells me that the reason people put these messages on groups is to tell others, 'I have done my bit.' The same applies to greetings on festivals and other occasions. Dare I say that this is a need for validation? Because the effort to send a message directly to a person and to a group is exactly the same.

My way: I never ever send a greeting or condolence message on a group address. It will always be a personal call, note or email to a personal ID.

Make an effort: I learnt another lesson about making an effort in relationships. Some years ago, when our son Rahul got married, I got a letter from a school friend. He was junior to me in school. We are good friends but not very close. The letter was a one-pager, hand-written, to thank me for the invitation and explaining why he could not attend the wedding. The point that blew me away was that this friend was at that time the chairman of one of the largest corporate groups in south India and the country. I reflected on the letter and how it made me feel (remember—the need to feel wanted?). The letter hit me hard with an important message. It struck me that if that person could make the time to write a personal note to me then I had no excuses not to do the same with my friends.

My way: From that day on I made it a point to write personal hand-written notes to people close to me on important occasions. Interestingly, the response from my friends has been very consistent—they are touched by the gesture. One very old friend actually sent a hand-written note back to me saying he had got out his ink pen after decades to reciprocate. A student whom I met a couple of years after listening to my final lecture told me that he picked up this idea from my class. When he wrote a letter to his father, he said his father was moved to tears by the gesture.

Make an excuse to connect: We live in a fast-paced world. Social media platforms, apps and smartphones give us the illusion that we are connected to people, when actually the opposite is becoming a reality. There is no substitute for the personal touch. The personal touch fulfils almost all the needs that I have enumerated above as basic to us humans.

My way: I have a list of 200 to 250 people who matter to me. I make it a point to make a personal call to them on their birthdays and wedding anniversaries and for condolences. If I cannot call them personally, I send them a personal message by email or text. It is now a given with many of my friends to expect a call from me on their birthdays. I often hear them say that they are amazed at the unfailing regularity with which I remember these dates year after year. My reply is simple—it is no thanks to me. Thanks are due to Apple or Microsoft for their calendars and reminders. I only need to decide that the call is important to me. (Remember, we have the tools. It is only about how to use them, that is, if we want to use them at all.) As I see it, this is one way of telling myself that people are important, and I get a reason to keep in touch. A nice five to ten-minute chat is a great way to keep a bond going. We are living in a world of distractions, and these are activities that fall into the category of 'important but not urgent' and get pushed aside. It is all about priorities. Mine are clear.

Show you value your associations: In our big fat Indian weddings it is customary, almost mandatory, for a video and a picture of the guest with the bridal couple. The guests are obliged to stand with the couple, smile for the picture and then walk off to the dining area. I thought about this when my son Rahul got married and asked myself what I could have done differently. How could I tell my friends that the effort they made to accept our invitation and their presence meant a lot to all of us in the family?

My way: After the wedding I printed the photographs and sent each of my friends their picture from the wedding with individual thank-you messages scribbled on the back. Even today, years after the wedding, many friends recall the gesture fondly.

Appreciate the effort of others: People always want to feel important and wanted. We often take people for granted, especially those close to us.

My way: My wife Thangam made some ground rules in our home as our children were growing up. At meal-times there would be no watching TV. When mobile phones came in, the ban was extended by me to say that there would be no phones at the dining table. The logic was that someone has taken the effort to make the food and we need to respect that. It also, of course, helps us concentrate on the food. This practice continues even today, about thirty-five years after it started. Now our grandchildren bear the brunt of this rule in our house! I am sure many of us will find it difficult to follow this rule.

Do not ignore, pay attention: We seem to have lost the basic courtesy of looking at people when they are talking to us. Oftentimes when I talking to someone, I find them looking into their mobile phone. I stop talking. The common response I get is—go ahead, I am listening. My reply is—you finish what you are doing and then I will talk to you. The message gets across and the phone is put aside. This happens in one-on-one communication in both personal and business-related contexts, in family and social gatherings and even in business meetings.

My way: How do you demonstrate to the person you are in conversation with that she is important to you? How do you give undivided attention in these days of distractions? As a rule, when I have guests at home my phone is on silent mode and I do not take any calls. When I visit someone, too, I ensure that the phone does not interrupt my visit. I believe I need to focus on the person in front of me. The irony is that when my guests visit me at my home, I give them my time and undivided attention, but they get on to their phones to talk to others. I have been toying with the idea of asking all guests to switch off their phones when they enter my house. Quite frankly, I have not had the guts to do it as of the time of writing this!

The mobile phone is a conversation pooper, and all of us need to be cautious about its use. It never ceases to amaze me to see a couple presumably on a date in a restaurant intensely engaged with their mobile phones. When I mentioned this to Rahul, he jokingly told me that I am a dinosaur and do not understand the youth of today. He said the couple were probably texting each other! Maybe he was not joking? We seem to be losing the ability to spend quality time with people.

My ways listed above are just a few of the items in my tool kit to achieve the particular goal of valuing relationships.

One final thought on helping us make the best of relationships, especially with those close to us and who matter. Any relationship is about give and take, and about having clarity on what is okay and not okay between individuals. I have found that just rejigging two terms that often crop up in associating with people can make a world of difference in creating healthy relationships.

Compromise is a term that often comes up, especially in close relationships—between spouses or partners, children and parents, close friends and colleagues. The word 'compromise' suggests concessions; giving up something to keep someone else happy; getting a less-than-desirable result. Essentially, there is a sense of net loss. I have found that a better way to approach relationships is to make *adjustments* to make them stronger or better. For me it is not about compromise but about adjusting to meet the other person's needs. I find this less troublesome.

Likewise, 'tolerance' is considered a positive trait that we should all possess. The word has its roots in 'tolerate', which implies putting up with something or someone that you may not necessarily like or approve of. In my understanding, there is an undertone of condescension in this. There is a sense of sacrifice, as with compromise. I have found that instead of tolerance, *acceptance* is a better word. Acceptance of another person's behaviour, personality and actions show respect and equality in the relationship.

Thus, in my relationships, I hope I adjust instead of compromise and show acceptance instead of tolerance.

To Sum Up

- Money cannot buy happiness. People can help you be happy.
- Focus on the quality of your interactions with people who mean something to you.
- Relationships influence your state of happiness and have an impact on both physical and mental health.
- Loneliness kills.
- Reflect on people who matter to you and set out your plan for how you would nurture and build your relationship with them.
- Physical connect is far better than virtual connect.
- Be aware of the downsides of the internet, mobile phones and social media and their effect on relationships.
- Our attention spans are dropping and this has an adverse effect on our ability to involve ourselves with people.

In 'The Origins of Happiness: The Science of Well-Being Over the Life Course' by the well-being programme at the Centre for Economic Performance at the London School of Economics, it is reported that the strongest factor predicting a happy adult life is not children's qualifications but their emotional health. The evidence shows that the things that matter most for our happiness and account most for our misery are our social relationships and our mental and physical health.[22]

I have shared some of the steps I have taken to strengthen my relationships. This has helped me find balance in relationships. You could use my steps and your own ways to find yours.

8

INVOLVE: FROM THE HEART

What Happened to Our Excellence?

India is a country that has been the cradle of civilization, knowledge and, importantly, excellence, in just about every sphere of activity. In fields ranging from architecture, construction, medicine, mathematics, metallurgy and science and technology to weaving, artisanship and philosophy, India had been the envy of the rest of the world thousands of years ago. Sadly, all this is a story, glory and legacy of the past. We know where we stand in the twenty-first century, after all the years of invasion, plunder and colonization.

We have become a '*chalta hai*' country. Anything goes. We have become a nation that will do as little as possible to get away with just what we need to do. Our indifference to commitments, obligations—contractual or otherwise—excellence, pride in what we do, is sadly now part of our national character. This is worrisome for the country in general and for you and the future generations in particular.

This brings me to the third **I—Involve**. Put your heart into what you do.

Jugaad—a Vice Made into a Virtue

If there is any one concept or quality that harms us most today, it is jugaad. This word has become a part of the social fabric and personality of India. Management gurus and academics write books about this Indian characteristic as if it is a great management asset. Jugaad has actually worked its way into the English lexicon. We Indians have, unfortunately, turned a vice into a virtue. The Oxford English Dictionary defines jugaad as 'a flexible approach to problem-solving that uses limited resources in an innovative way'. Academics and management pundits say jugaad is 'frugal innovation'. This certainly gives a sense of dignity, credibility and legitimacy to a completely avoidable and harmful trait or practice.

What really is jugaad? The academic definition makes jugaad a very necessary quality for a country like ours—frugal, innovation with limited resources, street-smart. We need to be aware and beware of this, because the ground realities are quite different from what these pundits say. In real life, as I and I am sure many of us have seen and experienced, the word jugaad has a different connotation. It is about working around the system, beating the system and breaking the law if needed, to get things done—as in 'we will do some jugaad'. I am not concerned with this interpretation at this juncture because this is a clearly undesirable quality.

The second and more common connotation is the one you should concern yourself about. You are probably already a victim of it. All types of product and service providers are constantly doing jugaad to fix problems. Typically, they are band-aid solutions to problems that should not have happened if the job had been done right in the first instance. It is a 'fix-it' approach. In management language, we can say it is not doing it right the first time and then fixing it the second time. I see this with students and professionals too. Typos in presentations, blind cut-and-paste jobs in reports and errors in spreadsheets are quite common. Look at our roads, buildings, services . . . We have become a nation conditioned to taking shortcuts. It is not just about beating traffic lights, cutting the roundabouts, going the wrong way on roads and one-way streets, or parking in no parking zones, but more importantly, it has pervaded almost every aspect of our personal and professional lives. Unfortunately, jugaad, the fixing of the problem, is seen as smartness. We glorify the poor uneducated guy who displays 'so much smartness using limited resources in an innovative way', and this is the so-called greatness of jugaad. We do not ask why the problem or error happened in the first place. This should be a matter of concern. This common attitude implies that we are not fully involved in what we do. It suggests a degree of casualness or even indifference to quality and excellence. We need to put our heart into what we do.

Passion, Good. What About Obsession?

The words typically used to describe a situation of being completely involved and putting your heart in what we do include 'commitment', 'passion', and even 'obsession'. Generally, when we talk of passion and obsession, the former is seen as a positive quality while the latter is not necessarily a desirable characteristic. For the purposes of this chapter, I will use obsession as a positive trait in a particular context. Let me explain.

I once heard a talk on achieving excellence by Geet Sethi, a five-time World Professional Billiards Champion. He made an interesting point about passion and obsession, saying that passion is not enough to take one to great levels. He said one has to be obsessed to be a champion. As I listened to him, my mind went back to about thirty-five years earlier, and I could relate exactly to what he was saying. In my college days I was a sportsman of decent capability and achievement. I played badminton and represented my university and state at the national-level championships. During my student days in engineering at IIT Bombay, there were many days when, after my practical classes in the afternoon, I would take the long haul by bus and local train from the IIT campus into town to play the local tournaments. After about two hours of commute each way and waiting for my match, which would often get delayed, I would return late to the campus, around midnight. The IIT routine those days was quite gruelling, with regular exams and assignments. There was no question of bunking classes or the class tests the next morning at eight thirty. It was a tough routine. But despite the tough academic and exam schedules, through my five years at the IIT, there was hardly a day when I was not on the sports field or in the badminton court in the evenings, working out or practising. This kind of routine made me proud of myself for my passion for and commitment to the game. Like many students of my time, with all my commitment to the game we would also have our flings, drinking binges, late-night parties and the like.

In my final year I was selected for the trials for the All-India Universities team. This was a big deal, because in those days the national team would have quite a few players from university teams. At the selection camp in Gwalior, we would all work out hard during the day and then fool around in the evening. I remember clearly that while many of us would sit up chatting, one person would quietly leave the crowd early and retire for the day. No late nights; no sitting around with the gang, as a good, healthy well-adjusted twenty-year-old would. We all noticed him, his actions and his commitment. The same person went on to win the national championship that year. In 1980, he became the first Indian to win the All-England Open Badminton Championships. He was ranked world's number one player the same year. His name was Prakash Padukone.

Thirty-five years later, sitting in a seminar in Thiruvananthapuram, and listening to Geet Sethi, I clearly understood the difference between passion and obsession. I was passionate about badminton. Passion was important, and it took me to a good level. I needed to be obsessed to get to the next level of greatness. I missed it. Prakash got there.

Let us look at passion and obsession in the context of our goal of happiness. I summarize the meanings of passion and obsession.

Passion is connected with intense emotion and feeling. When we feel passionate about someone or something we give it our whole and invest our emotions in it.

Obsession is about the domination of one's thoughts or feelings by a persistent idea, desire or thought that continually preoccupies one.

From my perspective, obsession is about focus and single-minded purpose. It need not always be for some big goal or objective. I take you back to the earlier chapter about 'Brand You'. Something that defines you is what you become obsessed with. It could be something as simple as having a tidy room or not allowing an untidy report to leave your office. I reiterate, I am referring to obsession in a positive context—of wanting something intensely. This obsession drives us to performance and achievement. It is not in the context of making us paranoid, where it becomes counter-productive, affecting not only our performance but also our emotional well-being.

If we look into the lives of the great people in various fields—art, science, music, technology and business—we will find that they went beyond passion to being obsessed with some idea or goal to get to where they did. Let us look at some of the most successful entrepreneurs in recent times whom I am sure we will be able to relate to. Steve Jobs of Apple. Bill Gates of Microsoft. Elon Musk of Tesla. Jeff Bezos of Amazon. Phil Knight of Nike. Or look at some of the great musicians, artists, writers and stage personalities. There are enough biographies on them. If there is a common trait to each of them it will be their obsession to pursue a goal or an idea that got them to where they finally reached.

What has obsession got to with jugaad? Everything. We Indians have to change our mindset to not settle for mediocrity. We have to get out of the '*chalta hai*' attitude that has permeated all levels of our society. We have to stop taking shortcuts, whether on the road or in our activities. We need to get injected with some amount of obsession for excellence and pride in what we do. We need to be obsessed with not settling for second best. We need to put in our best at all times, whatever the outcome. This can happen if and only if we are actively involved in whatever we do.

Steve Jobs was well known for his obsession with perfection and attention to detail, among other things. One can debate whether a CEO of a multi-billion-dollar company should get into the nitty-gritty the way he did. I will not argue about this quality of his, though under his leadership Apple broke records in just about all measures of corporate performance. Let us look at the one example of his single-minded pursuit of excellence and perfection—his obsession in designing the Apple Store. In Walter Isaacson's excellent biography of Steve Jobs, Larry Ellison, CEO of Oracle, says about Steve Jobs: 'He was obsessed by every detail of the aesthetic and the service experience.' Jobs delayed the planned roll-out of the store by three to four months to reconfigure the layout of the store to fall in line with his philosophy. There are also stories of how Jobs laboured over the correct shade of grey for the restroom signs and the amount of attention he paid to getting the right shade of Italian stone for the floors, at a cost of up to ten times more than it otherwise would have been.

As I write this chapter, one name that has become a household name the world over, thanks to the Covid-19 pandemic, is Zoom, the video conferencing platform. Zoom, the last kid on the block in this field, has become the market leader by a long shot. Born in China, CEO Eric Yuan, a former CISCO employee, started Zoom in 2011. His estimated personal net worth, at $15 billion, puts him in the top 400 richest Americans. Interestingly, he is reported to have moved to America in 1997 after eight failed attempts to obtain a visa! This is persistence, involvement, maybe even obsession.[1,2]

Remember, I have been talking about obsession as a positive trait that spurs one to achievement. This kind of obsession in turn gives us a sense of satisfaction and happiness in what we do. There is, obviously, a thin line between passion, commitment and obsession. If the obsession gets too much, then it would become unhealthy, unproductive and even destructive. Just like too much or too little of stress is not good, we each need the right dose of obsession. You cannot have this right amount of obsession if you do not have—yes—Involvement.

Multi-tasking—the Other Red Flag

After jugaad, the second vice that has been made into a virtue is multi-tasking. Thanks to the many ways of connecting simultaneously on the phone, laptop, tablet and so on, we have numerous distractions popping up through the day. One shifts from working on a report or project or reading to an email to checking WhatsApp, Twitter, Instagram, Facebook and who knows what else. This, in today's jargon, is called media multi-tasking. My view is that this is not just happening with the younger generation but even with older people. In meetings I see people doing all sorts of things except listening to the speaker. It appals me to see senior executives sending messages during working hours—from jokes to philosophy to news. When I ask them why they are not focusing on the job they are supposed to be doing and getting distracted instead, they come up with the new mantra—we multi-task. This is a 'skill' which people are proud of.

A majority of people who spend their time going back and forth between tasks believe that their multi-tasking is making them more efficient. However, many studies are finding that multi-tasking is no longer a skill to brag about, but a habit to worry about. These studies suggest that multi-tasking causes us to actually make more mistakes, retain less information, and changes the way our brain works. Individuals almost always take longer to complete a task and do so with more errors when switching between tasks than when they stay with one task.[3] More mistakes mean not doing it right the first time. Welcome to jugaad now to fix it!

Being Involved—the Challenge

What I see as a matter of concern is the increasing inability of people to focus and concentrate on a single job or task. It is not just at the workplace that the negative ramifications of productivity and performance are evident. I see the problem as more deep-rooted. The need to keep switching between media is almost a compulsive behaviour. It has become an addiction. I have not understood why people in cinemas, sports grounds, live shows and social get-togethers are constantly on their mobile phones sending messages, updating

Facebook posts, taking calls and so on. I wonder why people would pay money, spend a lot of time to come for an event and yet not be fully present physically and mentally at the show. Our ability to stay involved with a task and give it our 100 per cent is getting limited. The irony is that we have lost the ability to do what our forefathers preached thousands of years ago—be in the here and now.

In the last chapter we spoke about technology and social media and their effect on relationships. All studies seem to point to the fact that this trend is not good for the individual and for society at large. Let us see what else is happening to us.

If you have read up to this point in this chapter without looking at your mobile phone, your mail, TV or any other device, then it would be a miracle. I said that obsession is about focus and single-minded pursuit of a goal. This would imply paying attention to what you are doing and not getting distracted. The world around us, unfortunately, is not helping much in this direction. According to research, our attention span has markedly decreased in just fifteen years. In 2000, it was *12 seconds*. Fifteen years later, it had shrunk significantly, to *8.25 seconds*.[3]

What does this mean? Imagine trying to get someone to listen to you—as a salesperson, in a professional context, social or family situation—and do what you want them to. It could be anything. It is almost impossible to get someone's attention and hold it. In the same way, you also find it very difficult to stay with one task or thought for any significant time. Think of how much attention you really pay to what your spouse, partner, parent, child or friend is saying. An average office worker checks his or her email inbox thirty times every hour—yes, every two minutes. They will pick up their phones more than 1,500 times per week, amounting to three hours and sixteen minutes a day. On average, users will read at most 28 per cent of the words on a web page during a visit, with 20 per cent a more likely expectation. The average page visit lasts less than a minute, and users often leave web pages within twenty seconds. According to a 2010 study, nearly 47 per cent of our waking hours is spent thinking about something other than what we are doing. It's not unusual to find your mind wandering when you should be focused on something.[4]

Look around you and see what's happening. These are some of my experiences.

- In the middle of a sales call the salesman takes a call.
- While the plumber or service provider is doing his work he leaves his work to take a call. Or worse, he is working and talking. Any surprise then that when he leaves the tap is still leaking or the work is not done properly?
- When the purohit is doing a puja his mobile rings and he takes time out to answer the call.
- You are with your doctor and he takes a call in the middle of your consultation.
- You are with a friend, spouse, child or anyone. In the middle of a sentence you are broken off because the other person's phone rings. Your chain of thought is interrupted.

The list goes on and on.

'We Are Like That Only'

I ask myself—why is there so little involvement in what we do? Why have we, in India, become so indifferent to excellence and pride in our work? Why do we not put our heart and soul in what we do? There is much written and discussed on these matters by experts. Let me share my views based on my interactions over the years with many students and youngsters, including some of the best that this country can produce.

In an earlier chapter I talked about the youth today wanting to take the elevator and not the stairs. The need is for quick if not instant gratification. This need has seeped into our DNA, where our goal is not about what we should do but how soon will we get what we want. Students want guarantees when they pass out of college—about their job, the role, the career path, the salary and the perks. The job gets broken up into tasks that need to be completed to get to our desired goal. I have hardly sat in on a presentation in my class or in the corporate world where there have not been some typos or data errors. I sincerely hope there are none in this book, because in almost every book I have read in recent times I have come across at least one typo. This situation—of lack of rigour—is even more serious amongst service providers such as building contractors, electricians, plumbers, masons, carpenters, service engineers and so on. Very rarely have I ever seen anyone do the job right the first time. When it is time to redo the job, the reply is almost always 'no problems, I will do it'. *Jugaad zindabad!* The servicer actually thinks he is being helpful and honest since he willingly comes back to fix the problem. He is ensuring customer satisfaction. He does not even think it relevant to ask himself why he did not do the job properly the first time. I do not think I have seen a repairman tidy up the site where he has worked and leave it neat for the customer. He would do it only if he took pride in his work, which should include the cleaning of his workplace after he leaves it. He must be involved.

My Way

Multi-tasking is a good ability, but not necessarily a good trait at all times. I have understood that it is essential to build your ability to focus and be in the present. I realize that this will not happen intuitively any longer thanks to the various distractions that have been discussed in this chapter. One has to work to a plan consciously to pay attention. I constantly remind myself to be careful so as not to fall into trap that I see others falling into. The questions I ask are:

- When was the last time you spent time with your parents, partner, children, friends, without the phone by your side?
- Can your family go out to dinner without carrying their mobile phones? Can all of you engage with each other for thirty minutes to an hour without anyone touching the phone?
- How long have you been able to talk to your family without looking at your mobile or the TV?
- How long can you watch a full film or TV serial without looking at your phone or computer?
- Have you been able to sit through a show, play, concert or game without having to see your phone?
- Have you even been able to go for a walk or to the gym without carrying your phone?
- Can you think of working on your report or assignment for twenty minutes without wanting to see your email or messages?

You can add your own points to this list.

To Sum Up

We need to shun jugaad in this country. This has driven us to mediocrity, more than we realize or is good for us. Many of our engagements and activities have become transactional. A student submission. A report. A repair. There is no emotional involvement. It's just a job that has to be done.

Involvement will not happen by chance. You have to commit to be involved in what you do to make it a part of you. The feeling of a job well done and the conviction that you gave it your best imbue your activities with meaning and become, consequently, a source of happiness. India desperately needs you to inculcate this quality.

Steve Jobs sums the issue up aptly:[5]

> We made the iPod for ourselves, and when you are doing something for yourself, or your best friend or family, you're not going to cheese out. If you don't love something, you're not going to go the extra mile, work the extra weekend, challenge the status quo as much.

In short,

> Put your heart into whatever you do.
> Give it your 100 %: relationships, interactions, job, hobby … Don't settle for anything less.

9

IMBIBE: ABSORB, ASSIMILATE, LEARN

IN THE LAST THREE CHAPTERS we have seen how the rapidly changing world is impacting us in ways, both positive and negative. We have looked at some of the challenges that make happiness elusive. We have so far discussed three steps that can move us on the path to happiness consciously.

If we look at what has really changed our lives over these last few years, I find it comes down to two big trends—technology and globalization. Technology has offered us huge comforts and conveniences, without a doubt. It has also changed the way we live and behave. We have seen how technology has impacted the basic social fabric of our lives in the context of social behaviour and norms (think mobile phones, social media, low attention spans). In many ways, technology has led to globalization; to huge opportunities for individuals and corporations, making the planet a borderless world. It has also created an open battleground where competition is virtually infinite and where getting and staying ahead in the race is tough (think pressure to perform, big stakes, taking shortcuts, losing integrity, jugaad).

Let us now look at the impact these changes have on us as individuals. Whether you are a marginal farmer, small businessman, trader, doctor, corporate head honcho, a scientist, academician, an artiste, politician or bureaucrat, there is one thing you can say for sure. Tomorrow will not be the same for you as today. The global trends and changes will most definitely impact you personally and professionally. You have to be ready for them and work to deal with them. There is no possibility that you can maintain the status quo.

Live as if you were to die tomorrow. Learn as if you were to live forever. – Mahatma Gandhi

This saying has never been more relevant or important than for the times we live in now.

This brings us to the fourth I—**Imbibe**.

Dictionaries define 'imbibe' as to drink something, especially alcohol. 'Imbibe' also means 'to absorb or assimilate' (especially ideas or knowledge). It is in this second context that I talk about imbibing. Keep absorbing. Keep assimilating. Keep learning.

Learning—There Is No Final Destination

In his bestselling book *Homo Deus*, historian Yuvan Noah Harari says,

> 'Traditionally life has been divided into two main parts: a period of learning followed by a period of working. Very

soon this traditional model will become utterly obsolete, and the only way for humans to stay in the game will be to keep learning throughout their lives, and to reinvent themselves repeatedly. Many, if not most humans, may be unable to do so.'[1]

In the constantly changing world, advances in technology, along with the trend of professions being taken over by computer algorithms, artificial intelligence and automation, have significant implications on two fronts for people—the prospect of not just being unemployed but also of being unemployable. Automation with cars that drive themselves, machines that can read X-rays and algorithms that answer customer queries are some of the realities of the changing world. A 2017 McKinsey report on what the future of work means for jobs, skills and wages predicts the following for 2030:[2]

- As much as one-third of the United States workforce could be out of a job by 2030 thanks to automation.
- The proportion of the workforce that will be displaced by automation will be 30 per cent at a fast rate of automation and 15 per cent at a medium rate. This translates to 800 million and 400 million people, respectively.
- The report also predicts that at a fast rate of automation, up to 14 per cent of the workforce (375 million) will have to change their occupational category.

All predictions point to the future being highly dynamic and uncertain in terms of knowledge, skills and employment. In the US, the median number of years that wage and salary workers have worked for their current employer is currently 4.6 years, according to a 2018 Economic News Release from the Bureau of Labor Statistics.[3] There will be a demand for people to be flexible and adaptable in different roles and/or in different career fields. The skills that people learn at the beginning of their careers are unlikely to be what they will need even for the same job in the future. Upskilling, reskilling and lifelong learning will be the name of the game.

As students, we heave a sigh of relief when we graduate from what we think and hope is the final port of call for our education. If the reports I have just cited are any indication of tomorrow's world, you can figure out for yourself as to how much of what you have learnt and worked on will be relevant twenty years from now. Since the world twenty years from now is likely to be vastly different from what it is today, it is almost impossible to know what to learn or teach today that will be of relevance then. What we are seeing is that there is virtually no final destination for formal education and learning.

Implications: Types of Learning

It will be imperative for each one to

- Have a strong continuous-learning mindset.
- Have a plan for learning.
- Ensure and make a habit of continuous learning.

In my experience, I see that we do not pay much attention to the types of learning and their relevance and impact on our effectiveness as individuals, which in turn lead to our well-being. I see that we often tend to believe that gaining knowledge is equal to learning. Obviously, knowledge is the starting point. The questions we need to ask are:

- Why are we learning?
- Do we need to learn?
- What do we need to learn?
- How effective is our learning?

Learn to Learn; Learn to Teach

At an individual level, I find that there are two dimensions on which learning becomes important for a person.

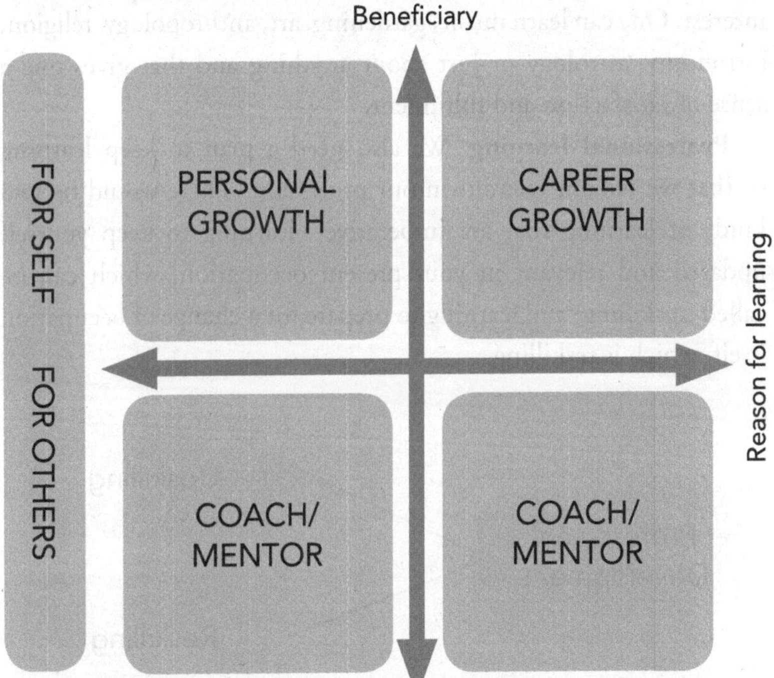

I have put the learning objectives in the above matrix. On the horizontal axis we have the reasons for learning. Learning could be for personal development or for professional development. On the vertical axis we have the net beneficiary of the learning. Are you learning for yourself or to help others? This sounds confusing, so please bear with me.

The objectives or intended outcomes of the learning are indicated in the boxes.

Personal learning: This is largely focused on personal development. The topics would include interpersonal communication, personal growth or any other subject of personal interest. One can learn music, gardening, art, anthropology, religion, astronomy, astrology or just about anything and that gives one a sense of satisfaction and fulfilment.

Professional learning: We also need a plan to keep learning so that we remain relevant in our profession. There would be two kinds of learning that are imperative—learning to keep yourself updated and relevant in your present occupation, which can be called upskilling; and learning to prepare for a change of occupation itself, which is reskilling.

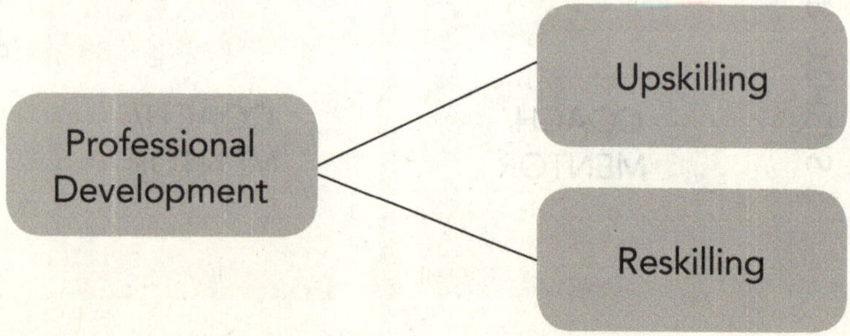

As we saw in the prediction of the work scene of the future, we have to be prepared not only to be continually updating ourselves in our current jobs (upskilling) but must also be prepared to shift careers and occupations due to the changing environments (reskilling).

A natural consequence of this new world is the need for us to be equipped to learn throughout our lives. We must learn to learn. There will be no end to it.

The other demand for learning comes from the fact that over the years our roles keep changing, and with that comes the need for us to have the adequate knowledge and skills to perform our new roles well. In whatever field we may pursue, at various times we would need to be a parent, friend, supervisor, manager and leader. One important component of our effectiveness is our ability to transmit our knowledge and wisdom to others so that they may perform effectively. In the process, what really happens is that we need to become good teachers. To be a good teacher it is not enough to have knowledge. We need to be able to use the knowledge as relevant and communicate it so that others grasp what we know. This has brought me to the realization that we all need to learn with two broad objectives in mind:

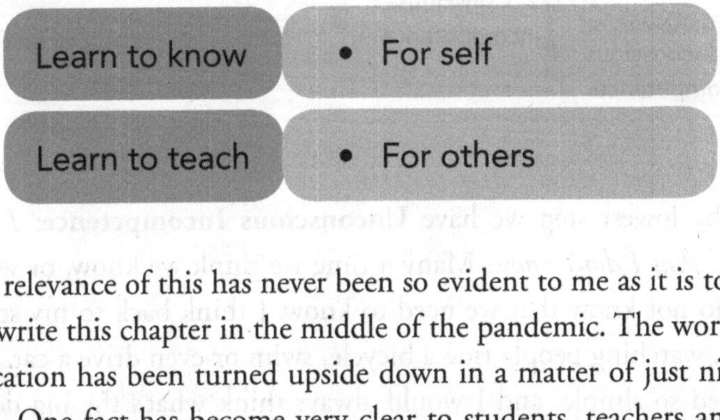

The relevance of this has never been so evident to me as it is today, as I write this chapter in the middle of the pandemic. The world of education has been turned upside down in a matter of just ninety days. One fact has become very clear to students, teachers and to the academic fraternity as a whole. Teaching online is a completely different ball game as compared to teaching in a physical classroom. Teachers have to equip themselves for a total paradigm shift in teaching and now have to upskill and actually learn how to teach all over again. With all the technology at our disposal, knowledge alone is of no use in the present circumstances.

The Learning Process: Four Stages of Competence

Conceptually, it is easy to talk of the importance of continuous learning and personal development. People from all spheres of life will talk about the importance of learning. However, what we need to do is to take a cold, hard look at how well we actually do on this dimension of learning as we move on in life.

There is a popular framework for stages of learning—it is based on understanding our level of incompetence and our awareness. We typically go through four stages of knowledge acquisition.

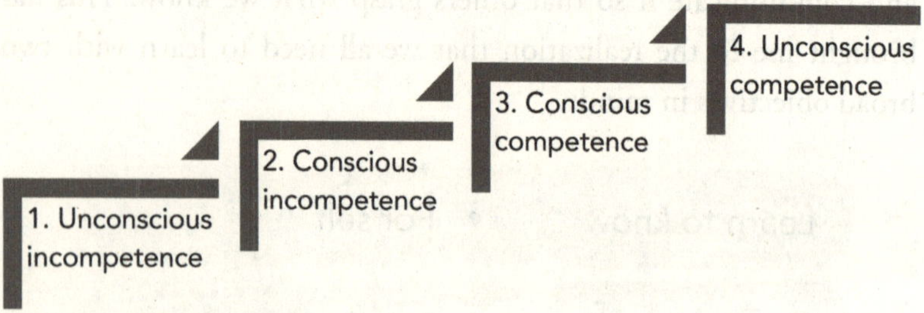

At the lowest step we have **Unconscious Incompetence**: *I don't know that I don't know.* Many a time we think we know, or worse, we do not know that we need to know. I think back to my school days, watching people ride a bicycle, swim or even drive a car. It all looked so simple, and I would always think what's the big deal. I understood what the deal was when I got on to the bicycle and into the water for the first time! In such instances when we are exposed to something new which we thought was quite obvious or simple we actually open our minds to learning. This leads to the next stage.

I moved to the next stage of **Conscious Incompetence**. *I know that I do not know.* I realized that I did not know how to ride a bicycle or swim. Cycling or swimming are not things that come naturally and have to be learnt. This is the stage at which one can be open to learning.

I then moved on to the third stage, where I had to be very aware of my cycling or swimming. It was a laboured effort. I had moved to **Conscious Competence**.

Finally, after some practise and experience, I could ride a bicycle and think of many other things at the same time or get into the water without swimming along the sides so that I would not sink. I moved to the stage of **Unconscious Competence**. At this stage, *what I have learnt becomes a habit.*

The point to note from all this is that learning happens only when we acknowledge the second stage—we know that we do not know. This sounds simple, but it does not always work out.

Challenges to Learning

How many times have we heard someone say he will never learn! Or, why does someone not learn or want to learn? There is another well-known framework that can help assess how receptive a person might be to learning. This categorizes the situation of an individual with respect to knowledge and awareness. We have four possible situations, as depicted below.

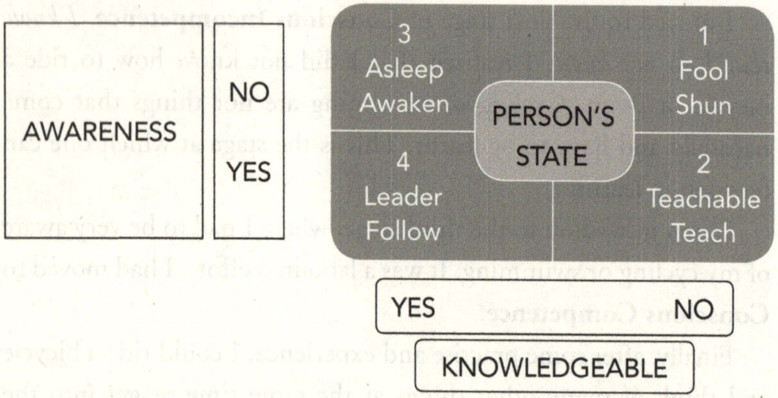

This can be described very well in the following manner:

1. He who knows not and knows not that he knows not, he is a fool, shun him.
2. He who knows not and knows that he knows not, he is teachable, teach him.
3. He who knows but knows not that he knows is asleep, awaken him.
4. He who knows and knows that he knows is a leader, follow him.

Ask yourself which box you fall into. Your receptivity to learn will only happen if you fall into box 2, when you know that you do not know. This is the equivalent of the state of Conscious Incompetence mentioned earlier. Similarly, in your role as a teacher, check out which quadrant your learner belongs to so that you know the teaching demands.

The next question is—how we get to looking at ourselves and admitting that we do not know? I see three major qualities—the 3 H's—that help us learn:

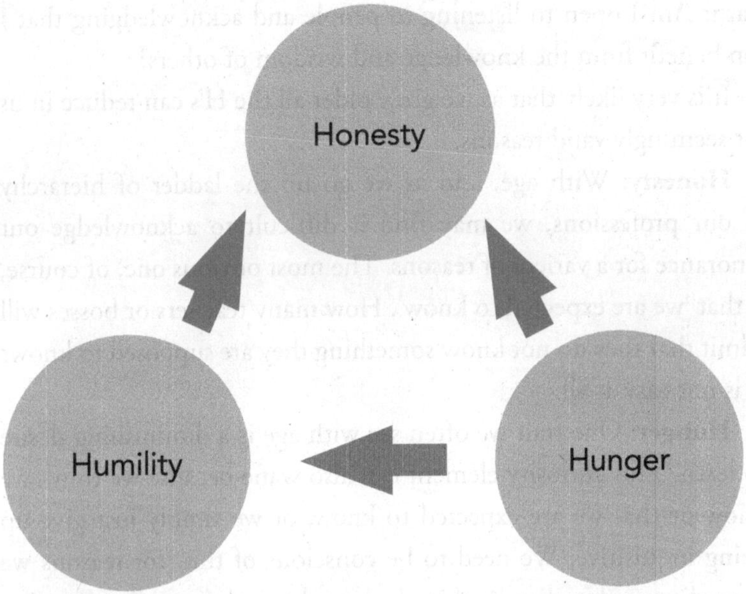

Honesty: I must first admit I do not know if I am open to learning. This makes me teachable (see above). I need to be honest. It is easy to be honest when you are young or in a domain which is alien to you and others do not expect you to know much about it. No one will think the less of you for it. In fact, they would appreciate your honesty when you say, 'I do not know.' What happens as we grow older and are expected to know?

Hunger: The best learners are little children. Every parent and adult who spends time with kids gets worn out by their questions. For everything you say, there is a 'why?' They are hungry to know more. Whatever you say is not good enough for them. Are you hungry for knowledge and to learn? This essentially comes from curiosity and inquisitiveness.

Humility: Finally, am I humble enough to acknowledge and admit to myself and others that I do not know and that I need to learn? Am I open to listening to people and acknowledging that I can benefit from the knowledge and wisdom of others?

It is very likely that as we grow older all the H's can reduce in us for seemingly valid reasons.

Honesty: With age, and as we go up the ladder of hierarchy in our professions, we may find it difficult to acknowledge our ignorance for a variety of reasons. The most obvious one, of course, is that 'we are expected to know'. How many teachers or bosses will admit that they do not know something they are supposed to know? It is not easy at all.

Hunger: One trait we often see with age is a diminishing desire to learn. This curiosity element can also wane because we think we know or that we are expected to know, or we simply just give up being inquisitive. We need to be conscious of this, for reasons we have discussed earlier in this chapter about the rapidly changing world scene and the risk of obsolescence.

Humility: I believe this is the most important quality, which in many ways is a superset of the above two qualities. Ego and arrogance can be huge blocks to learning. We need to be open to listening and learning from anyone, anytime.

> If you are not willing to learn no one can help you.
> If you are determined to learn no one can stop you.

One other factor to look out for is the tendency to maintain the status quo. Doing things the same way over and over again puts us in a comfort zone and we stop thinking. I see this is especially true with organizations where processes were put in place at a point in time when they were relevant. These processes are then on auto-mode and often do not achieve the desired results. Two such examples stand out in my mind because we all experience it on a regular basis.

a) Many years ago, hotels started the concept of a 'welcome drink' at the time of check-in. This was considered an 'excitement feature' (in marketing jargon) and was in fact a good feature. Over the years, this became almost standard practice in hotels. In many hotels the welcome drink is a sugary, sickly sweet, coloured drink, which many guests actually reject. This is a good way by which I keep myself amused in the lobby of a hotel, by watching the number of people who do not take the welcome drink. The welcome drink seems to have lost its value. I wonder if hotels track the number of guests who do not take the welcome drink and learn something from it. It is part of their standard operating procedure (SOP), whether it is relevant or not.
b) The second common example is of the large number of impersonal automated messages one gets on one's birthday or wedding anniversary. This was again unique and interesting; it is part of a strategy for companies to build relationships with their customers. This has now degenerated into spamming the customer's mailbox. I would really be interested to know how many customers really value this flood of emails. It's just a whole lot more of emails to be deleted. The mails and messages are irritants.

Learning Stops When We Stop Thinking and Questioning

I do not want to go into the detailed methods of how one can learn. There is obviously no one right way. Very broadly, there is a learning related to technical knowledge or is discipline-specific, where one needs a certain rigour and structure for knowledge dissemination and assimilation. The other important part of learning and skill development relates to attitude, behaviour and relationships. I consider this as a very important part of the skills we need at all stages of our lives, irrespective of our chosen line of work. A lot of the skills involve what is called soft skills or life skills. We are really never formally taught soft skills. We are generally left to our own devices and are expected to pick them up as we grow up. Soft skills are what goes to strengthen the third I—Interact. Soft skills help us connect with people and help in our personal growth. Each one of us must ensure that we are equipped with all-round skills and competence and not just the technical or professional skills required in our fields.

I have one easy way of picking up soft skills. Almost every minute of our waking day we are interacting with people. At home we interact with our family, at work with colleagues, and in shops, restaurants, taxis, buses and trains with counter people, and with call centres. We interact in person, over the phone, by email or even on the internet or web. While many interactions may be neutral, I have seen that every day I will have at least one interaction that leaves an impression on me—positive or negative. I then analyse such interactions and try and understand what the other person did or did not do that made me happy or unhappy. The rest is simple. I then tell myself what I need to do or should not do when I deal with others. Every positive impression builds a relationship and every negative one weakens it. Lesson learnt. My best teachers have been vegetable vendors, taxi drivers, waiters in restaurants, small-time service people and the like. I am sure each one of us has had experiences with some people that have made a lasting impact. Every individual, however high or low profile, can make an impact and be a teacher. If we can accept this, imagine the opportunities we have to learn, and, more importantly, the opportunities we have to make a positive impact on people we come in contact with in our personal and professional lives and to strengthen our relationship quotient. This is what Jan Carlzon of Scandinavian Airline System (SAS) called 'Our Moments of Truth'. For me, my daily life is the learning platform for soft skills. The examples from my daily-life experiences form the basis of many of my discussions even in my strategy classes and workshops.

All this reminds me that there is a need to keep your antennae up and to be always receptive to learning because you can be taught by anyone at any time. A large part of learning actually happens outside of classrooms. When my daughter Rohini was about eight, I learnt an important lesson in time management and planning at our dining table. As a general family rule, we could not say that we did not like any item of food made at home. We were expected to have at least one helping of what was made. The option for a second helping was left to the individual. One evening I saw Rohini eat up an item that she did not like very early in the meal. Surprised, I asked her why she ate it so fast since I thought she did not like it. In a very matter-of-fact eight-year-old way, she said, yes, she did not like that dish. So she thought it best to eat it first, get it out of the way and enjoy the rest of the meal; that would be better than dreading having to eat that dish at the end in any case and losing out on the process of enjoying the other dishes. This was brilliant. Because this is what one learns in time and activity management, where experts explain this in a 2 × 2 matrix, as below:

	Like to do	**Don't like to do**
Don't need to do		
Need to do		

The common trap is to do what you like to do even if you do not need to do it (top-left quadrant). We procrastinate doing things we need to do but do not like, until they become emergencies (lower-right quadrant). What time management experts teach in seminars was taught to me by an eight-year-old at the dining table. A very unlikely classroom and teacher.

This was a big learning for me. There is really no right time or place to learn, and everyone can be your teacher. The world is your classroom. All you need to do is to keep your eyes, ears and mind open, and the opportunities are limitless.

You are never too young to teach.
You are never too old to learn.

Learning does not stop when you get out of university. School and university education are more about knowledge gathering and assimilation than about true learning. It is only when knowledge can be translated into action does it become true learning. The hard reality is that schools and colleges can never teach you all that you need to know to make your journey in life in whatever field you may choose. These institutions lay a foundation and act as best as trailers of things to come. I often find young people graduating from B-schools very anxious about their campus placements. They are especially hung up on what they call 'role'. My suggestion to them is fairly standard. It is almost impossible to project where a person will be thirty years from the day he/she sets out from the university campus. The journey has just too many variables for every person, without exception. You can trace the lives of many successful people and check for yourself whether where they started out in their twenties as a career was a good indication of where they would end their careers in their fifties or sixties. I ask them to think of the first job as a continuation of their college learning process. One significant difference in this learning is that someone pays handsomely for you to learn! It's only when one goes into a job with that frame of mind that I find true contribution and personal growth happening.

In this context I am reminded of my friend Venky Mysore. He was a career insurance person. Venky was a fast-tracker with a leading American insurance company. He came to India to set up the company operations in the early 2000s. A chance meeting with a professional acquaintance resulted in his changing his path completely. The professional acquaintance is co-owner of an India Premier League franchise (IPL). Within a couple of months of the meeting, Venky found himself as the CEO of Shah Rukh Khan's Kolkata Knight Riders (KKR), running a cricket franchise. Twenty years of his insurance career was a story of the past. Today, about ten years down the road, Venky has made KKR an international brand and is also CEO of Shah Rukh Khan's film production company Red Chillies Entertainment. Venky Mysore says if anyone had told him this was in store for him two months before he entered the film production and entertainment business he would have said it was impossible. Today, not only is he firmly entrenched there, KKR is now an international brand and probably the most profitable Indian T20 cricket franchise too. Venky has demonstrated two I's very clearly on his path to success—Imbibe and Involve. He shifted gears, he learnt the new business and has given it his 100 per cent. He is also a very happy person and strong on the other I's too.

A Final Thought on Learning

Knowledge by itself is of no use if it cannot be used effectively. Knowledge must result in wisdom for the seeker of knowledge. The process of moving from knowledge to wisdom is beautifully brought out in a saying by Adi Shankaracharya:[4]

'The right guru gives soul and depth to knowledge, for mechanical knowledge is not enough; knowledge must lead to understanding, understanding to contemplation and contemplation to the wisdom to differentiate between the eternal and ephemeral.'

Confucius said it differently:

By three methods we may learn wisdom: first by reflection which is noblest; second by imitation which is easiest, and third by experience, which is bitterest.

We live in a complex and dynamic world. It is virtually impossible to know everything. I have learnt that the skill of an individual, like that of a good doctor, lies not in finding a solution but in defining the problem. We should learn to define problems. I have found that very often, when the problem is understood and defined properly, the solutions are generally obvious. Going back to what I said in the beginning, know the why. The what and how depend on the why. We should know whom to approach to solve our problems. The doctor analogy works well here too. A good diagnosis results in fairly obvious prescriptions and treatments. The judgement is at best in the nature and extent of dosages.

To Sum Up

The mind is like a parachute—effective only when it is open.

- In the coming times, learning will not be an optional, nice-to-do activity but will be continuous and essential for personal growth and well-being.
- We will need to keep learning for both personal and professional development.
- With age and rank, it becomes tougher to say, 'I do not know.' Lack of knowledge and skills can be disconcerting, resulting in anxiety, depression, fear and so on. In short, stress. There will always be the need to be honest and open about your lack of knowledge and show a willingness to learn.
- We need to have the three H's to keep an open mind: honesty, hunger and humility.
- I expect it will be easier for the coming generations to say 'I do not know' than for mine, for whom the pace of change was much slower than it is now.
- On the flip side, the slow pace of change allowed us to be happy—a luxury that seems to be eluding the younger generation.
- A good way to learn is to teach. Teaching forces one to not just know a subject but also articulate and communicate one's knowledge to an audience. In the process, the teacher has to structure his or her thoughts and relate to the student. I have found this to be an excellent way of improving one's own knowledge and skills. This is important, because there are various types of learning needed to be effective in the various roles you will play in your life—as partner, spouse, parent, adult, team member, team leader, professional.

We now move to the last I of our GPS.

10

IMPACT: MAKE A DIFFERENCE

THE HOLLYWOOD COMEDY DRAMA *The Bucket List* (2007) features two outstanding American actors, Jack Nicholson and Morgan Freeman. The story revolves around two terminally ill men who decide to complete a wish list of things they would like to do before they 'kick the bucket'. The wish list takes them to various places around the world. In one scene, as they sit outside the Pyramids in Egypt, Freeman tells Nicholson:

> Ancient Egyptians had a beautiful belief about death. When their souls got to the entrance of heaven, the gods asked them two questions. Their answers determined whether they were admitted or not.
>
> 1. Have you found joy in your life?
> 2. Has your life brought joy to others?

This in essence sums up the whole path and journey of our lives and brings us to the last component of the GPS for happiness.

The fifth I: **Impact.**

This chapter in a way closes the circle which I began drawing at the start of this book to give the reader a direction for Happiness and Success. I will limit the context of impact to its role in my search for happiness and success. I submit that impact is the final decider on the Happiness–Success quotient for an individual. It answers the question as to whether one's journey in life has had any meaning or relevance at all. At various points in our life journey we need to ask of ourselves, 'What am I really doing and what have I really achieved? Have I made a difference at all?'

In short, what impact have I made?

How does one answer these questions?

This would depend on what achievement and impact mean to an individual. It would depend on the individual's definition of success and happiness. This calls for defining one's personal KRAs (key result areas), and doing it with clarity. It is quite ironical and paradoxical that we spend a lot of our time and energy in our professional lives visioning, fixing objectives and targets, planning strategies for our organization, implementing these strategies and periodically reviewing targets and performance. How many of us do the same in our personal lives?

As Freeman puts across very simply—one important KRA for each one of us should be, 'Has my life brought joy to others?'

Value and Impact

In my marketing strategy classes we discuss the concept of customer value. A sale can only be made when the customer perceives she gets value from the product. A sale is a give-and-take transaction. The customer gets value when she believes she has got more than she has given. The customer gets the product and its features, the service, reputation, brand image, and a whole lot of other tangible and intangible benefits. Similarly, she gives a price, uncertainty, time, opportunity and other tangible and intangible factors.

In simple terms:

VALUE = GET > GIVE

In the same manner, we need to check if we have delivered value as a person.

On the lines of the same equation above:

IMPACT = GIVE > GET

We have made an impact when we have given back to people, our community and society, more than we have taken from them. This is especially important for you, dear reader. Since you are reading this book, you would be part of a very tiny proportion of fortunate people in the world, and certainly in our country India, who have had the luxury of living a life beyond having to think of just *roti, kapda, makaan*. For most readers of this book, chances are that, thanks to the good fortune of your birth, you would have crossed the first three stages of Maslow's hierarchy pyramid. You would not have to worry about your basic needs. You are most likely in the upper part of the pyramid, focusing on esteem and self-actualization. It is very easy to be unaware of and disconnected from the world of a large majority of the population that lives in poverty and tough financial conditions.

> I do have one big regret. I left Harvard with no real awareness of the awful inequities in the world—the appalling disparities of health and wealth and opportunity that condemn millions to lives of despair. – **Bill Gates @ Harvard 7 June 2007**

This is what Viktor Frankl means when he talks of having a sense of meaning in life. We have to look at ourselves and see what we have done or are doing that goes beyond just thinking about ourselves. We need to continually ask ourselves if we are sensitive to what is happening in the world around us and what our role and contributions are beyond our jobs and making a living.

I'll Do it Tomorrow; Too Small to Make a Difference

When one is young one is naturally, and rightly, busy with the priorities of building a profession and career and moving through various stages of the family life cycle. Thus, one may not have the time or energy to think beyond oneself and one's immediate family. We may get into important-but-not-urgent-so-do-it-tomorrow traps and put off doing things that lie beyond our own immediate needs and personal gratification. This is quite understandable.

Another factor that can add to the inertia of contributing is the feeling that 'I am too small to make a difference'. This, I believe, is the greater danger. What is important to note is that no one is too small and no act too little or insignificant if it makes a difference to another person. The important requirement is a sense of purpose and the desire to help others. Every large deed started small. Every small deed is big for the receiver who needs it.

> A journey of a thousand miles starts with the first step. – Lao Tzu

I will share three seemingly small incidents which, as I look back, have made a profound impact on me, and have remained with me over the years.

1. During my college days in the 1970's, India was a country of severe shortages. Even the well-off could not easily access the essentials of daily life, including milk, sugar, rice, wheat and bread. My father was a senior officer in the Indian Navy. I used to see him take a loaf of bread to office two or three times a week. When I asked him why he did this, he told me that he was taking it for a clerk in his office. The young, hierarchy- and rank-conscious chap that I was, I asked him why as a boss of the office he was taking a loaf of bread for a clerk. My father told me that the person was a bachelor, suffering from cancer and did not have anyone to take care of him. He said, 'I am only doing what little I can to make his life easier.'
2. Years later, my father settled down in the outskirts of Coimbatore in Tamil Nadu. He used to drive into the city centre every day. He put a board on his vehicle that read, 'Kovai Pudur to Coimbatore, free rides.' His logic once again was simple. He was travelling alone. There were many people waiting for public transport. It was no problem for him to give lifts to people. For him it was just natural to do what he did. In the process he made many friends. There were many write-ups in the local press about this retired naval officer giving free rides to people in his Maruti van.

3. I learnt another lesson from Rahul when he was just ten years old. At that age he had to change two buses to get to school and back each day. Those were the days well before we had mobile phones and a good school bus system in Bangalore. I certainly could not afford a driver to drop him to school every day. Rahul would use the city's bus system. He would have just about enough money for the bus and maybe for some tuck in school. One evening he did not get back home at the usual time. The delay got us worried, and we had no way of knowing where he was. We went to the two bus stops where he would take the buses and asked around. No news. We waited anxiously. Thankfully, he walked in home with his tie around his shoulder and his shirt sticking out of his shorts, as usual. We heaved a sigh of relief before showing our anger at his being late and not coming straight home from school. He told us what happened. At the bus stop where he had to change buses a person came to him saying he wanted some money since he had not eaten for days. This ten-year-old goes on to tell us that the man seemed really hungry and genuine. Rahul thought that if he gave him the money he could not be sure if the person would use it for food. So he took that man to a restaurant and bought him some food and ensured that the man ate. He had used up all his money and had to walk home from the bus stand, and that was why he was late. He left my wife and me both ashamed and proud.

By themselves these are not examples of any great acts of kindness or benevolence. But I can relate to them clearly based on the statement from Egyptian mythology quoted earlier—has your life brought joy to others? Each one of the above examples passes this test.

My learning on Impact is:

> Every act of kindness, however small, is big for the receiver who needs it.

The starting point for Impact is a belief that you want to and can do things that don't just benefit yourself. It starts by believing in something bigger than yourself. Standard theory and common sense will talk about having a purpose, finding something you truly believe in, finding your mission and so on. In my experience, not many of us have this clarity of purpose. I believe the important need is to decide that you have to go beyond the normal or ordinary and commit to making a difference. As you try different things, I have no doubt that you will find some initiative that you find fulfilling and satisfying. I have learnt through personal experience that you do not always need to have a great vision and passion to make a difference. In my case I stumbled upon an idea purely by chance, and that became a strong passion.

> 'Pursue something so important that even if you fail, the world is better off with you having tried.' – Tim O'Reilly

Make a Reality Your Passion: Vishwas Society for Mental Health, Thirty Years and Still Ticking

In 1991, a few people got together to be trained as lay counsellors to help people in emotional distress. There was really no plan as to what would happen after the training, except maybe do something for cancer patients and their caregivers. I and, for that matter, most of us who attended the programme had nothing whatsoever to do with counselling or mental health. The intensive training left a few of us deeply impacted about the importance of mental health and the urgent need for counselling. A group of us decided to take this to the next logical step. We formed an organization to offer free and confidential counselling services to people in emotional distress. Thus was born Vishwas, Society for Mental Health, purely by chance. The passion, the commitment, the involvement grew when we saw the need for such services in a high-stress world and the benefit our callers (we do not call them patients or clients) derived from us. As I write this chapter, Vishwas has completed thirty years of service. We have helped over 17,000 people. We have had over 350 people who have volunteered with us over these years. We have volunteers who have been with Vishwas for over twenty-five years. We have stuck to our core principles: we do not charge even a rupee to people who come to us for help and have never paid a rupee to people who offer their time as volunteers. Our callers are amazed that we spend hours listening to their problems and giving them emotional support. Their normal refrain is that they cannot believe that there are people who are willing to sit with them for hours and just listen to them without getting tired or impatient. The reason for our spending time with them is quite simple: we do not bill our time, so there is no pressure to maximize revenue.

The important lesson I have learnt from my experience with Vishwas is that you do not always need to have a passion to make it a reality. You can have a reality and it can become your passion. The one essential drive my colleagues and I have is the desire to make a difference. To do something that goes beyond ourselves. That's it.

Selfless Service: The Gurudwara Langar

Look around and you will find numerous people and organizations going beyond themselves to do amazing things. I believe that these are the people and institutions that make the world a good place to live in. The unsung, everyday heroes.

There are many people who do remarkable good through foundations and charity organizations. Writing a cheque is not very difficult for people who have a lot of money in the bank. The Giving Pledge initiative of Melinda and Bill Gates and Warren Buffet is just one of many such organizations which went one step more than just giving money. Not everyone is or can be a Bill Gates or a Warren Buffet. One good way to make an impact is to part with some of your precious and valuable assets to help others. What is our most prized asset? No, it is not money, because for the rich, giving part of their wealth will not make any substantial difference to their bank balance or lifestyle. Our most valuable asset is time. I have found that true impact is made and a sense of satisfaction derived when we give a part of ourselves to a cause through our time and personal engagement. That demonstrates genuine involvement.

One institution that has never ceased to fascinate me is the gurudwara of the Sikh community, especially their langar. A langar, in simple terms, is a free communal kitchen for all, regardless of race and religion. This is a feature one can see in gurudwaras all over the world. I would, however, strongly recommend that everyone makes a visit to the holiest of shrines for the Sikhs, the Golden Temple in Amritsar, and watch their langar operations. The kitchen feeds on an average 50,000 people every day of the year, with the numbers going up to 1,00,000 on important festivals. The langar operates 24×7×365.

The interesting fact is that about eighty to ninety per cent of the people who run the langar are volunteers. This is a place where one sees *seva* (selfless service) in its truest sense. The volunteers come from all cross-sections of society—rich and poor, men and women, children as young as seven or eight to people over seventy. From taking your footwear to washing the dishes and clearing the dining hall, they do it all, irrespective of their social and economic status in the world outside. If ever you are looking for an example of humility and selfless service on a large scale you will find it here. I found it fascinating just to sit outside the langar and watch the volunteers doing *seva* with a sense of passion and commitment that is hard to describe. The important point is that each of these volunteers makes an impact in his or her own small but significant way.

My Way

My one-line test of Impact that sums up a lot of what is said above:

> What have I done to leave the place better than I found it?

People who make a positive impact are role models. The opening scene in *The Bucket List* says:

> You measure yourself by the people who measure themselves by you.

There is no better way to say it.

To Sum Up

In Chapter 1 I spoke of Viktor Frankl's *Man's Search for Meaning*. A meaningful life that can lead to a sense of satisfaction and happiness is about connecting with and contributing to something beyond the self. The pages of achievements listed on resumes are only justifications for the salary you have earned or what you might be demanding. Ask yourself, what you are doing beyond earning your livelihood? What have you done to make life better for someone who is not as privileged as you are? Do you have a desire to do something for people who are not as fortunate as you are? Those are your true achievements.

It is heartening to see many young people getting into societal initiatives that go to helping the less privileged, the environment and civic issues.

Interestingly, thinkers and spiritual leaders cutting across religions and time periods have emphasized this aspect. It is only appropriate that this completes the steps one takes to achieving happiness. I will, therefore, leave it to these stalwarts to give you their message directly.

> Be the change you want to see in the world.
> – Mahatma Gandhi

> Rivers do not drink their own water; trees do not eat their own fruits; the sun does not shine on itself and the flowers do not spread their fragrance for themselves. We are all born to help each other. No matter how difficult it is . . . life is good when you are happy; but much better when others are happy because of you. – Pope Francis

In the end it's not the years in your life that count but the life in your years. – Abraham Lincoln

In life what matters is not what you gather but what you scatter. – Helen Walton

Thousands of candles can be lit from a single candle and the life of the candle will not be shortened. Happiness never decreases by being shared. – The Buddha

This wraps up my five I's or the GPS to happiness and success. In the final section we will look at some of the challenges we will face in achieving happiness. We will also attempt to validate and calibrate the GPS framework to allow you to create your own road map for happiness and success.

PART 3

11

THE CHALLENGE: TRANSLATING INTENT TO ACTION

We come to the last part of our journey to find success and happiness. The five I's for happiness and success have been defined in the previous chapters. As I wrap up this book, I will address three issues in this final part of the book.

- One of the challenges we face in personal and organizational situations is our inability to translate our noble intentions into action. We make promises, pledges and commitments and yet fail to implement them. These could range from the simple—like a pledge to exercise every day, or not to resort to unfair practices in our profession—to the more complex, such as having to make a trade-off between equally valid alternatives. I had briefly discussed this in the chapter on the first I: Integrity. We will discuss some of challenges we will face throughout our lives in this respect and the relevance of our GPS in helping us deal with them.

- I will then attempt to validate the five I's so that you are convinced about them. Since you are reading this chapter, I expect that you will have read the earlier parts of the book and subscribed to my GPS. I would like you to validate it through your own experience and judgement.
- Finally, I would like you to think about what you can do to set your own GPS for your life journey.

Dilemmas, Conflicts and Decisions

Life is one continuous process of problem-solving and conflict resolution. Every minute of our lives we are resolving some dilemma or the other. Thankfully, many of them are minor or small and we do not want to or need to expend much thought or energy on them. These are generally as simple as what to wear for an outing, what to eat for a meal, which movie to watch, what activity to pursue, which brand of product to buy and so on.

There will, however, be times when the situations are trickier and the answers not so obvious. These are the situations that can leave us with self-doubt and stress. The analogy I can use is arriving at a fork in the road and finding no indication of which road one must take to reach one's destination. I am sure that as Indians we can relate to this easily. At crucial points on a highway, we are often left guessing as to which road to take. Today on our road journeys we can get the GPS to tell us where to go. People of my generation wonder how we managed in our growing-up years without GPS and maps, which we now follow blindly. In our younger days we would pay attention to the directions given to us, note down the landmarks and stop often to ask people when in doubt to get where we wanted to go. Our life journey is not very different. We will reach a crossroads or fork where we would need to take a call on which way to go. There are no clear road maps or directions to help us navigate. In some cases it will not matter much which road you take. The cost and implications of taking the wrong road would be minimal. However, in some cases the cost of taking the wrong road can be high. This is where your personal GPS will kick in and help you navigate. In this section I will try and put in perspective the issue of dealing with such dilemmas and conflicts.

When we talk of dilemmas, difficult decisions and the need to make tough choices, two terms invariably crop up—ethics and morals. These are subjects that have been dealt with by great people across disciplines and over thousands of years. I will not be presumptuous to venture into that space. I will limit the discussion to the management of dilemmas and conflicts in a manner that makes us comfortable with what we do and leaves us at peace with ourselves. This is an important feature of our GPS.

Ethics: the discipline dealing with what is good and bad and with moral duty and obligation.

Morals: of or relating to principles of right and wrong in behaviour.

The challenge with the above definitions is the use of the words 'good', 'bad', 'right', 'wrong'. Whether something is good, bad, right or wrong is subjective and hence open to interpretation. Even what is moral or obligatory is open to interpretation, since there is nothing absolute about what these words stand for. These definitions are time-, person- and social-context dependent.

Typically, ethical dilemmas occur when there is no right or wrong way to deal with a situation. Unlike the dilemma of what to wear or which dish to order, some situations in our professional and social life that we find ourselves in involve a clash between personal values and professional and social norms or expectations. Sometimes there is a clear, straightforward answer to a situation or question. Most often, unfortunately, there is no clear-cut black or white path to resolving conflicts.

> It's never wrong to do the right thing.
> – Mark Twain

Mark Twain's statement is certainly simple, clear and powerful. The challenge is that right and wrong are not often clearly defined and lie in the eye of the beholder. Let me, however, simplify this philosophical issue for our purpose.

Situation 1: Apple iPhone

In 2016, Apple CEO Tim Cook would have been under tremendous pressure and probably intense criticism. Apple was locked in a big legal dispute with the FBI on a matter of privacy and data security. The FBI wanted Apple to help them gain access to the data in an iPhone used by a person suspected of involvement in a mass killing in California. The government contention was that cooperation in such cases could help prevent terrorist attacks against Americans.

Apple's contention was that if they agreed to do this, it might compromise the security and privacy of their customers in the future. They also worried about its implications with other governments, who could misuse this if it set a precedent. Apple senior executives, for their part, said their defiance was not a business choice. But cooperating with the government could lead to murkier situations internationally, especially in China, where officials have been pushing for greater control over the encryption and security of technology sold there. What should Tim Cook have done? Is he accountable to his customers or to his country?[1]

Situation 2: Fairness Creams

Fairness creams have been huge sellers in the Indian market and in other parts of the world. It is a cultural phenomenon in India that people value fair skin. Indian advertising in the past has emphasized the disadvantage of being a dark-complexioned woman and how opportunities open up if you are fair-skinned. As a marketing manager of a company selling these creams, is it right for you to advertise the benefits of buying your product to become fair? As a junior marketing executive of the company, what would you do if the campaign pitch conflicted with your personal value system? Is the job of the marketer to influence societal thinking and needs or to satisfy them? If you were to say that it is wrong, you might have to think again. Would the same yardstick then apply to tobacco, alcohol, junk food or aerated beverages?

In the above situations, there are really no clearly defined rights or wrongs for the individual or the company. These are 'dilemma situations', where the concerned executive has to take a call based on his or her personal compulsions and value systems. This happens to all of us at some time or the other in our personal, corporate, professional, political, civic and social lives. I will wrap up the discussions in this book with the following section, which is largely based on the work and writings of Rushworth Kidder, an American author and ethicist.

Moral Temptation vs Ethical Dilemma

When we have to make choices and take decisions, we could be faced with two situations: choosing between right and wrong and between right and right. When we have to choose between right and wrong there is really no major dilemma. If we choose the wrong, it is a conscious decision that one makes, knowing the implications of doing wrong, whatever be the compulsions. Of course, one is presumably willing to face the consequences of choosing the wrong. Daily instances of such behaviour are rampant—beating traffic lights, parking in no-parking areas, going the wrong way up or down one-way streets, using a false medical certificate, fudging accounts and inflating travel bills are the common ones.

However, we will often be faced with options, none of which are clearly right or wrong. Each of the options would have its own merits. This is when conflict arises and there is a dilemma. Having to choose between right and right is called 'ethical dilemma'. On the other hand, when we have to choose between right and wrong, we are in a situation of 'moral temptation'.

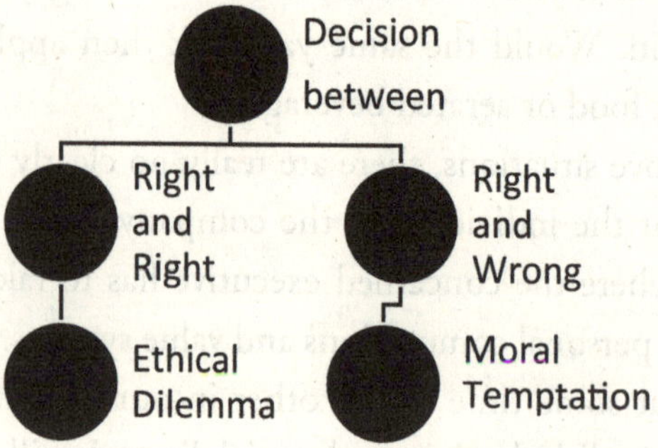

It is when we are in an ethical dilemma that our world of values, morals and principles come to our aid. This is not to say that the decision-making will be easy. It is more about being clear about the decision. What makes decision-making tough? Paradoxically, it is having strong values that makes the choice tough. It is easy to succumb to 'moral temptation' if one does not have a strong sense of values. In a way, this is linked to my first I—Integrity.

I do realize that I have said that integrity is the first I for me. I did not, of course, say it was easy to practise it, as many people with strong values and a strong sense of integrity have also found. However, what it does is to give you clarity and direction when faced with dilemmas and the strength and ability to live with the difficult choices you may have to make. Tough choices don't always involve professional codes or criminal laws. Nor do they necessarily involve big headline-sized issues. They are often in the domain of ethics, which involves principles, morals, values, codes of conduct and norms of behaviour.

Kidder describes four paradigms of ethical dilemmas:

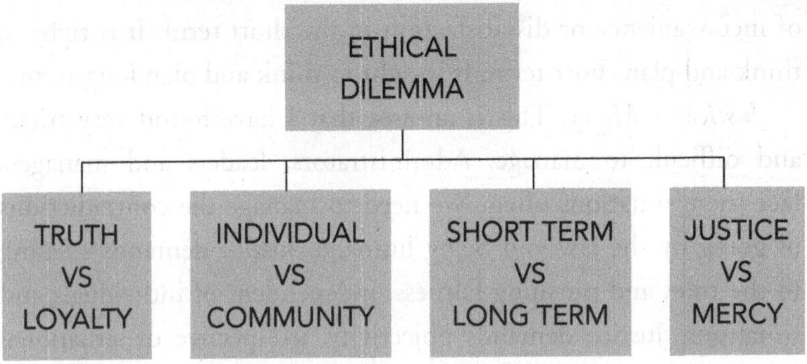

Let us look at the kind of situations that we can be faced with, which have no real right or wrong answer.

Truth vs Loyalty: Truth is about conformity to facts or reality. Loyalty involves allegiance to a person, organization, a body of people, a government or a set of ideas that one subscribes to. It is right to stand on truth. It is right to be loyal. If you are faced between telling the truth about a close friend who has violated a law and hiding it out of your sense of loyalty, what would you do? Your personal value system will have to provide the answer.

***Individual vs. Community*:** Is the interest of the individual prime or that of the community? The rights of an individual are to be protected, but what happens should the needs of the majority outweigh the interests of the individual? Communities lay claims on their members. We have discussed this in detail in Chapter 6 through the examples of G.R. Vishwanath and Adam Gilchrist. The situation of Apple's CEO Tim Cook described above also falls in this category. It is right and important to consider the individual. It is right to consider the community.

Short term vs Long term: This is a dilemma that we will be faced with often, especially when managing organizations and institutions. Managers would face short-term concerns that are associated with satisfaction of current and immediate needs. Long-term concerns involve future interests, which might mean some level of inconvenience or dissatisfaction in the short term. It is right to think and plan short-term. It is right to think and plan long-term.

Justice vs Mercy: This is an area that I have found very tricky and difficult to manage. Administrators, leaders and managers face these situations often. We need to manage the contradictions of going by the law and being humane. Justice demands sticking to the rules and pursuing fairness, independent of individuals and situations. Justice demands objectivity, irrespective of situational pressures. Mercy asks for being sensitive to individual needs and contexts. A poor student has not paid his tuition fees for months in an educational institution. As per the rules, non-payment of fees beyond a time frame calls for withdrawal of the student. Mercy tells you that the student has a genuine reason for not paying the fees and that removing him would be harsh. As an institution head, how much should one stretch the leeway for the student? It is right to be merciful. It is right to enforce justice.

In each of the above situations there is no one who can tell you what to do. Yet these situations are often the cause of stress and obstacles to happiness. Clarity as to who you are and what you stand for is of prime importance.

The Test: Right vs Wrong

There are three ways of being wrong:

- Violation of the law
- Departure from truth
- Deviation from moral rectitude

Rushworth Kidder suggests a simple and practical framework to test one's actions and help one in situations of moral temptation. Remember, moral temptation entails decision-making in a right-vs-wrong situation and is based clearly on the core values that each person possesses.

The Legal Test: Are you breaking the law? If yes, then it is a case of required adherence to the laws of the land. These are enforceable, as opposed to the unenforceable canons of moral code. Kidder postulates three other tests for right vs wrong.

The Stench Test: Does this course of action have about it an indefinable odour of corruption that makes you recoil? This is a 'gut test' and a 'gut level' determination. Always listen to your gut because it tests your internal code of morality at the psychological level.

The Front-Page Test: How would you feel if what you are about to do showed up tomorrow morning on the front pages of the nation's newspaper? What would your response be if a decision made in private suddenly became public?

The Mom Test: 'If I were my mother, what would I do?', or 'If Mom knew about this what would she think?' This is about the moral exemplar who cares deeply about you and means a great deal to you. Put yourself in the shoes of someone you look up to and think about what you are on the verge of doing.

To Sum Up

The reality of life is that we will continually face dilemmas and will need to resolve conflicts. Avoidance of dilemmas and conflict is near impossible. Good management is, however, helpful.

In this chapter I have attempted to address how understanding the type of dilemma you are faced with is helpful:

- It helps you separate right from wrong.
- It helps you cut through complexity and reduce confusion.
- It helps you cut out the extraneous stuff and get to the heart of the matter.
- Most importantly, it helps you to know what you are doing, understand the implications and be comfortable with your decisions and actions.

As I see it, for each one of us, ultimately, the journey is about:

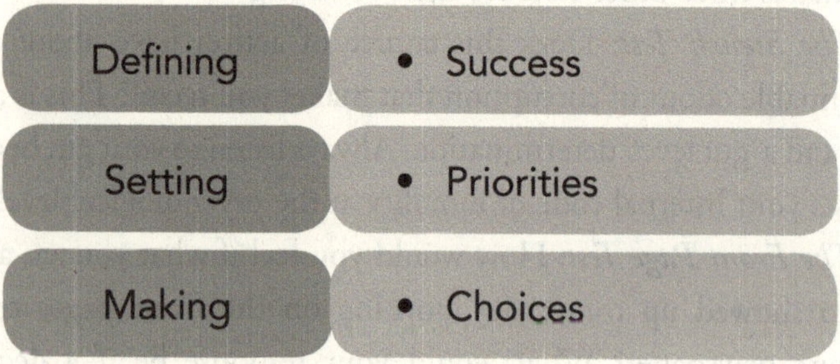

Through this book I have put together my thoughts and experiences to share my message with the younger generation as to how to achieve happiness, success and meaning in life. I hope the book gives you some pointers on what you could do. More importantly, I hope it gives you something to think about in the years that lie ahead. It is ultimately left to each one of us to chart our own journeys.

I will end with my favourite lines, a wonderful poem which sums up the onus on each one of us as individuals to choose our own paths to happiness and fulfilment.

THE MAN IN THE GLASS

When you get what you want in your struggle for self
And the world makes you king for a day
Just go to the mirror and look at yourself
And see what that man has to say.

For it isn't your father, or mother, or wife
Whose judgment upon you must pass
The fellow whose verdict counts most in your life
Is the one staring back from the glass.

He's the fellow to please – never mind all the rest
For he's with you, clear to the end
And you've passed your most difficult, dangerous test
If the man in the glass is your friend.

You may fool the whole world down the pathway of years
And get pats on the back as you pass
But your final reward will be heartache and tears
If you've cheated the man in the glass.

Author unknown

12

THE LITMUS TEST: VALIDATING THE 5 I'S GPS

I HAVE ELABORATED ON what I see as the basic ingredients to get us to the final goal of happiness—the five I's. It is time to check out and validate the model based on your personal experiences and judgement.

Think of anyone whom you know/have known as a role model and a happy person. This person must be reasonably close to you so that you know him or her personally.

Rate this person on a ten-point scale on the following qualities, with 1 for very poor and 10 for excellent.

HAPPINESS	1	2	3	4	5	6	7	8	9	10
INTEGRITY	1	2	3	4	5	6	7	8	9	10
INTERACT	1	2	3	4	5	6	7	8	9	10
INVOLVE	1	2	3	4	5	6	7	8	9	10
IMBIBE	1	2	3	4	5	6	7	8	9	10
IMPACT	1	2	3	4	5	6	7	8	9	10

How do you see your role model in the context of this framework?

13

CALIBRATION AND PERSONAL ROAD MAP

YOU CAN NOW CALIBRATE yourself on the five dimensions that can lead you on your path to happiness. Be honest with yourself—remember 'The Man in the Glass'. No one else matters. You can then get a context to work out a personal action plan to move forward.

HAPPINESS	1	2	3	4	5	6	7	8	9	10
INTEGRITY	1	2	3	4	5	6	7	8	9	10
INTERACT	1	2	3	4	5	6	7	8	9	10
INVOLVE	1	2	3	4	5	6	7	8	9	10
IMBIBE	1	2	3	4	5	6	7	8	9	10
IMPACT	1	2	3	4	5	6	7	8	9	10

Assessment of Myself and Action Plan

Based on how your self-evaluation goes from the exercise above, you can now put your personal five I's into action. On each of the five, you will assess your current situation, identify where you would want to head and what steps you will take towards it. For each of the I's you can plan on the following lines:

	I will stop doing.
	I will start doing.
	I will continue doing.

INTEGRITY			
INTERACT			
INVOLVE			
IMBIBE			
IMPACT			

14

A WRAP-UP

I HAVE PROVIDED in this book my GPS for happiness and success. As an aide de memoire for you, I recap some of the points discussed in the book.

The five I's can be placed in context, as shown below.

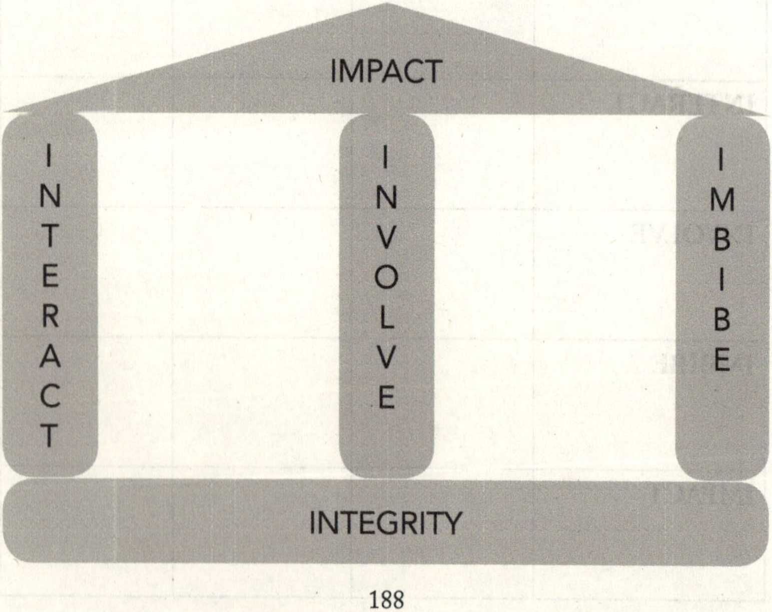

The core of our path to happiness is built on the foundation of Integrity. On this foundation, through Interaction (people and relationships), Involvement (giving your best) and Imbibing (always learning) you will hopefully get the satisfaction of making an Impact (making a difference). All this will give you a sense of happiness and meaning in life.

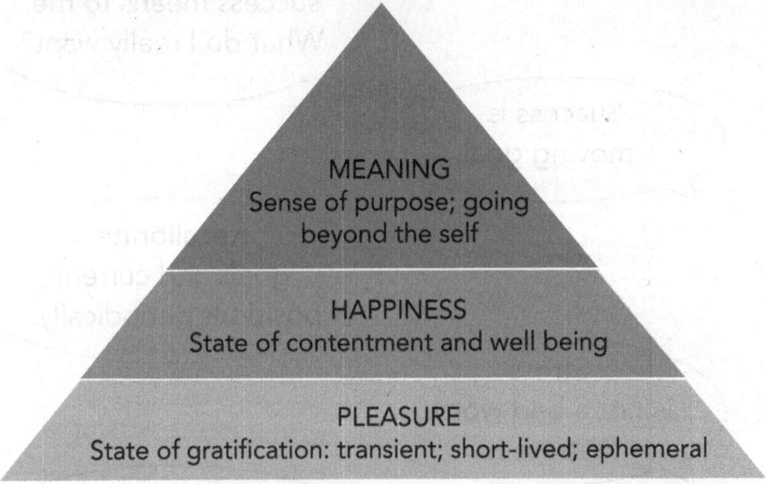

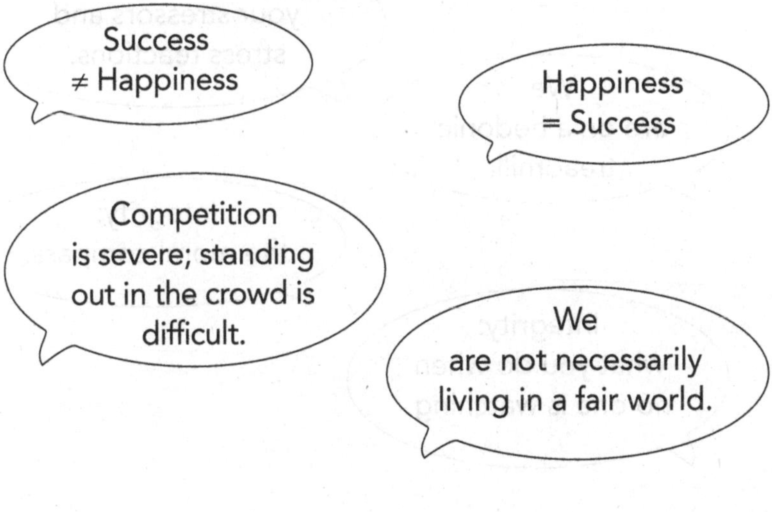

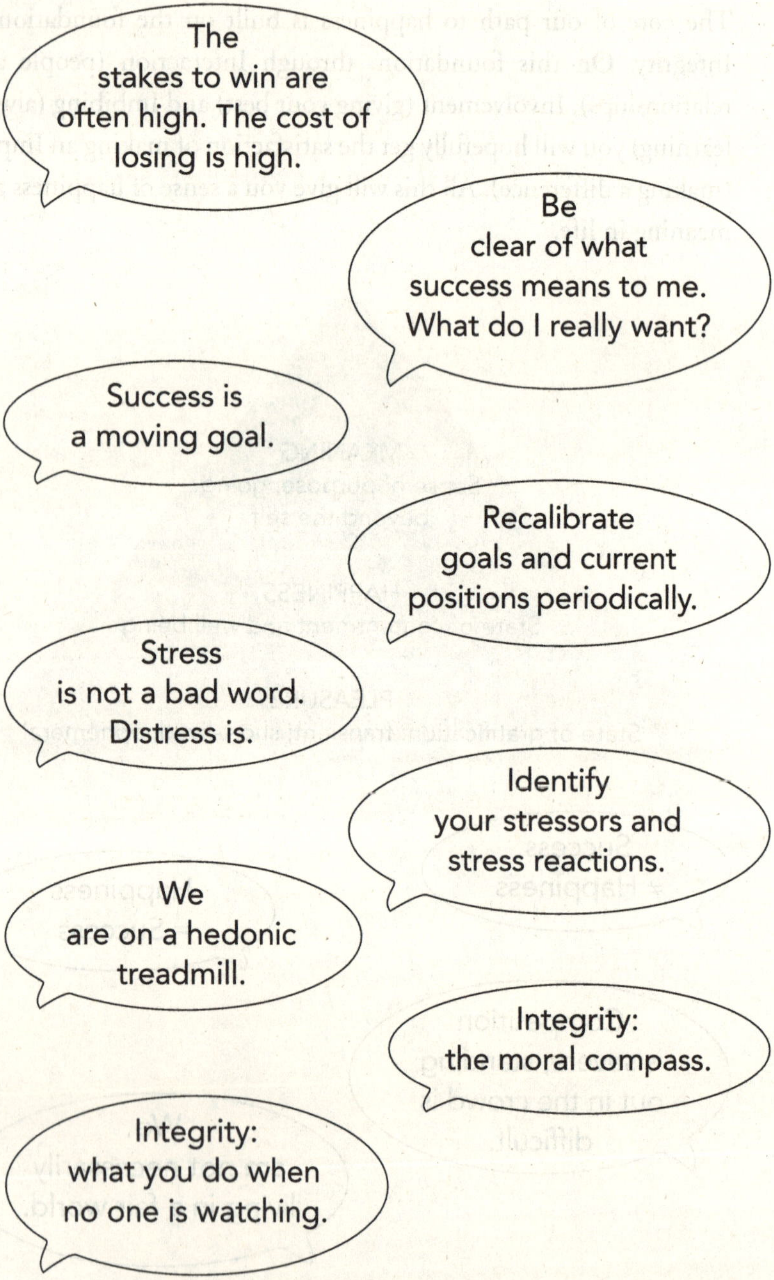
The stakes to win are often high. The cost of losing is high.
Be clear of what success means to me. What do I really want?
Success is a moving goal.
Recalibrate goals and current positions periodically.
Stress is not a bad word. Distress is.
Identify your stressors and stress reactions.
We are on a hedonic treadmill.
Integrity: the moral compass.
Integrity: what you do when no one is watching.

Interaction:
Money cannot buy you happiness. People can bring you happiness.

Involvement:
Always give your 100%.

Imbibing:
Absorb. Assimilate. Learn.

Imbibing:
never too young to teach. Never too old to learn.

Impact:
Bring joy to others.

Impact:
Have you left the place better than you found it?

Differentiate between ethical dilemma and moral temptation.

REFERENCES

2 HAPPINESS AND SUCCESS

1. Source: https://positivepsychology.com/hedonic-treadmill/, Accessed 28 December 2020.
2. Source: https://positivepsychology.com/hedonic-treadmill, Accessed 28 December 2020.
3. Source: https://greatergood.berkeley.edu/article/item/world_happiness_report_finds_that_people_are_feeling_worse, Accessed 28 December 2020.
4. Source: https://www.researchgate.net/figure/Average-Happiness-and-GDP-Per-Capita-1972-2016_fig20_323800048, Accessed 28 December 2020.
5. Source: https://www.caba.org.uk/help-and-guides/information/happiness-depends-mental-health, Accessed 29 December 2020.
6. Source: https://www.caba.org.uk/help-and-guides/information/happiness-depends-mental-health, Accessed 29 December 2020.

7. Source: https://www.stress.org/42-worrying-workplace-stress-statistics, Accessed 30 December 2020.
8. Source: https://childmind.org/article/is-social-media-use-causing-depression/, Accessed 30 December 2020.
9. Source: https://journals.sagepub.com/doi/full/10.1177/2167702617723376
10. Accessed 30 December 2020.
11. Source: https://www.developmentalscience.com/blog/2019/5/7/our-teens-are-more-stressed-than-ever, Accessed 30 December 2020.
12. Source: https://economictimes.indiatimes.com/magazines/panache/heart-attacks-on-the-rise-among-30-40-year-olds-diabetes-hypertension-are-contributing-factors/articleshow/66997025.cms, Accessed 30 December 2020.
13. Source: https://www.ncbi.nlm.nih.gov/pmc/articles/PMC6902359/, Accessed 30 December 2020.
14. Source: https://en.wikipedia.org/wiki/Suicide_in_India#cite_note-5, Accessed 30 December 2020

3 THE PRESSURE TO PERFORM

1. https://backlinko.com/facebook-users, Accessed 7 February 2021.
2. https://www.statista.com/statistics/260819/number-of-monthly-active-whatsapp-users/ Accessed 7 February 2021.
3. https://backlinko.com/instagram-users, Accessed 7 February 2021.
4. https://www.apa.org/monitor/2019/01/gen-z, Accessed 7 February 2021.
5. https://www.forbes.com/athletes/#2f0f8fbe55ae, Accessed 7 February 2021.

6. https://www.indiatoday.in/sports/cricket/story/virat-kohli-100-forbes-2019-list-worlds-highest-paid-athletes-lionel-messi-cristiano-ronaldo-neymar-federer-1546924-2019-06-11, Accessed 7 February 2021.

4 WINNING AT ALL COSTS

1. Source: https://list25.com/25-biggest-corporate-scandals-ever/, Accessed 31 December 2020.
2. Source: https://www.forbes.com/sites/jackkelly/2020/02/24/wells-fargo-forced-to-pay-3-billion-for-the-banks-fake-account-scandal/?sh=22b5f9b542d2, Accessed 8 February 2021.
3. Source: https://www.cbsnews.com/news/ranbaxy-whistleblower-reveals-how-he-exposed-massive-pharmaceutical-fraud/ Accessed 8 February 2021
4. Source: https://leftlanenews.com/chevrolet/gms-top-powertrain-exec-fired-over-india-emissions-scandal/, Accessed 8 February 2021.
5. Source: https://www.fraud-magazine.com/2018Top5Frauds/, Accessed 31 December 2020.
6. Source: https://www.bbc.com/news/business-46267868, Accessed 8 February 2021.
7. Source: https://www.thisismoney.co.uk/money/markets/article-8460299/Here-12-fraud-scandals-rocked-business-world.html, Accessed 9 February 2021.
8. Source: https://hbr.org/2010/04/envy-at-work, Accessed 9 February 2021.
9. Source: https://www.psychologytoday.com/us/blog/hide-and-seek/201408/the-psychology-and-philosophy-envy, Accessed 9 February 2021.

10. Anita Raghavan, *The Billionaire's Apprentice,* (Hachette India, 2013), p. 23.
11. Source: https://www.britannica.com/biography/David-Petraeus, Accessed 15 September 2021.
12. Source: https://economictimes.indiatimes.com/news/international/world-news/solitary-confinement-in-prison-was-like-being-on-vipassana-involuntarily-rajat-gupta/articleshow/68668782.cms?from=mdr, Accessed 15 September 2021.
13. Source: https://www.nytimes.com/2015/09/24/business/international/volkswagen-chief-martin-winterkorn-resigns-amid-emissions-scandal.html, Accessed 15 September 2021.
14. Source: https://www.nytimes.com/2019/04/15/business/winterkorn-volkswagen-emissions-scandal.html, Accessed 15 September 2021.

6 INTEGRITY

1. Source: https://www.thehindu.com/news/national/sex-with-minor-wife-is-rape-says-supreme-court/article19838085.ece, Accessed 9 February 2021.
2. Source: https://www.dlsweb.rmit.edu.au/Toolbox/knowmang/content/ethics/values_statement_enron.htm, Accessed 4 January 2021.
3. Source: https://mission-statement.com/wells-fargo/, Accessed 4 January 2021.
4. Source: https://www.volkswagenag.com/en/group/strategy.html, Accessed 4 January 2021.

7 INTERACT

1. Source: https://www.simplypsychology.org/maslow.html, Accessed 5 January 2021.
2. Source: https://journals.sagepub.com/doi/abs/10.1111/1467-9280.00415,
3. Accessed 5 January 2021.
4. Source: https://news.harvard.edu/gazette/story/2017/04/over-nearly-80-years-harvard-study-has-been-showing-how-to-live-a-healthy-and-happy-life/,
5. Accessed 5 January 2021.
6. Source: https://www.ted.com/talks/robert_waldinger_what_makes_a_good_life_lessons_from_the_longest_study_on_happiness?language=en, Accessed 5 January 2021.
7. Source: https://qz.com/1413576/loneliness-is-bad-for-our-health-now-governments-around-the-world-are-finally-tackling-the-problem/, Accessed 5 January 2021.
8. Source: https://www.forbes.com/sites/neilhowe/2019/05/03/millennials-and-the-loneliness-epidemic/?sh=1978a2e37676, Accessed 5 January 2021.
9. Source: https://www.jchs.harvard.edu/blog/the-rise-of-the-single-person-household, Accessed 5 January 2021.
10. Source: https://www.apa.org/members/content/holt-lunstad-loneliness-social-connections, Accessed 5 January 2021.
11. Source: https://www.forbes.com/sites/angelauyeung/2021/01/26/cause-of-fire-that-killed-tony-hsieh-still-unclear-investigators-cite-carelessness-but-will-not-rule-out-intentional-act/?sh=221929d74a70, Accessed 12 February 2021.
12. Source: https://www.forbes.com/sites/angelauyeung/2020/12/04/tony-hsiehs-american-tragedy-the-self-destructive-last-months-of-

the-zappos-visionary/?sh=5fad124a4f22, Accessed 12 February 2021.

13. Source: https://journals.sagepub.com/doi/full/10.1177/0265407519836170, Accessed 7 January 2021.
14. Source: https://journals.sagepub.com/doi/full/10.1177/2167702617723376, Accessed 7 January 2021.
15. Source: https://childmind.org/article/is-social-media-use-causing-depression/, Accessed 7 January 2021.
16. Source: https://www.forbes.com/sites/alicegwalton/2013/01/22/jealous-of-your-facebook-friends-why-social-media-makes-us-bitter/?sh=5257113f35cc, Accessed 9 January 2021.
17. Source: https://expmag.com/2019/03/jealous-of-your-facebook-friends-youre-not-alone/,
18. Accessed 9 January 2021.
19. Source: https://www.forbes.com/sites/alicegwalton/2017/06/30/a-run-down-of-social-medias-effects-on-our-mental-health/?sh=271acea92e5a, Accessed 9 January 2021.
20. Source: https://economictimes.indiatimes.com/magazines/panache/happily-divorced-indian-women-are-breaking-the-stigma-around-separation-like-never-before/articleshow/67704287.cms?from=mdr, Accessed 9 January 2021.
21. Source: https://www.ashleymadison.com/en-us/, Accessed 10 January 2021.
22. Source: https://www.mckinleyirvin.com/resources/digital-divorce-a-guide-for-social-media-digital/how-social-media-affects-marriage/, Accessed 10 January 2021.
23. Source: https://www.prnewswire.com/news-releases/big-surge-in-social-networking-evidence-says-survey-of-nations-top-divorce-lawyers-84025732.html, Accessed 12 January 2021.
24. Source: https://betzlawfirm.com/how-social-media-is-affecting-marriage-divorce/, Accessed 12 January 2021.

25. Source: https://www.caba.org.uk/help-and-guides/information/happiness-depends-mental-health, Accessed 9 January 2021.

8 INVOLVE

1. Source: https://www.forbes.com/profile/eric-yuan/?sh=4f9eb29f61bf, Accessed 11 January 2021.
2. Source: https://en.wikipedia.org/wiki/Eric_Yuan, Accessed 11 January 2021.
3. Source: https://www.wyzowl.com/human-attention-span/, Accessed 11 January 2021.
4. Source: https://appliedpsychologydegree.usc.edu/blog/to-multitask-or-not-to-multitask/, Accessed 11 January 2021.
5. Walter Isaacson, *Steve Job* (Little, Brown and Company, 2011), p. 407.

9 IMBIBE

1. Yuval Noah Harari, *Homo Deus: A Brief History of Tomorrow* (Vintage, 2017), pp. 380–81.
2. Source: https://www.mckinsey.com/featured-insights/future-of-work/jobs-lost-jobs-gained-what-the-future-of-work-will-mean-for-jobs-skills-and-wages#, Accessed 15 January 2021.
3. Source: https://www.bls.gov/news.release/tenure.nr0.htm, Accessed 15 January 2021.
4. Pavan K. Varma, *Adi Shankaracharya: Hinduism's Greatest Thinker* (Tranquebar, 2018).

10 IMPACT

1. Source: https://www.thebetterindia.com/53531/golden-kitchen-10-things-didnt-know-langar-golden-temple-amritsar/, Accessed 15 January 2021.

11 THE CHALLENGE

1. Source: https://www.nytimes.com/interactive/2016/03/03/technology/apple-iphone-fbi-fight-explained.html, Accessed 6 February 2021.
2. Rushworth Kidder, *How Good People Make Tough Choices: Resolving the Dilemmas of Ethical Living* (Harper Perennial, 24 November 2009).

INDEX

ACKNOWLEDGEMENTS

FOR A BOOK OF THIS NATURE it is impossible to thank everyone who has made it possible. I have learnt from almost every interaction with people over the last fifty-plus years, as far back as I can remember. Thanks to all the numerous friends, colleagues, acquaintances and the people whom I don't know and who don't know me but have taught me important lessons in my life's journey.

To my students in my strategy classes, it has been gratifying to know that the Final Lecture was one of the best you had attended in your institute. It often left me wondering what you all were doing in the other sessions which I always believed were the juicy ones! You were the ones who gave me the push to think of the final lecture as a book, which was finally nailed by my classmate. Thanks Vasantha for giving me a framework for this book.

My years with Vishwas has taught me to be sensitive and aware of the good fortune that many of us are bestowed with and that has allowed me to bring some meaning and happiness into the lives of others in some small ways. I owe this to my colleagues and callers who have been sources of inspiration and have constantly reinforced the importance of having a meaning in life.

Pradeep Reddy, your long phone call full of energy and encouragement after reading my first few chapters made me believe that this book might actually get published. Thanks.

Sridhar Balan—I will never be able to thank you enough for so willingly and promptly directing me to HarperCollins. I owe you much.

Krishan Chopra—most people told me that publishers can take anywhere from a few weeks to many months to respond to a concept or outline of a book. I was all set for the long haul. I could not believe it when I got your mail within just six days informing me that the book was on and you would confirm the contract. All this was based on a few pages of the introduction to the book from an unknown name and a rookie author. You have spoilt me—you have made publishing a book by a reputed publisher look easy. Thanks so much, Krishan.

To the HarperCollins team, it has been a delight to work with such a professional and competent group of people. The movement of ideas and views at great speeds have been amazingly productive and energizing. Thank you, Suchismita, for your patience in managing this first-time author so well. The ball was always in my court. You kept me on my toes!

Sanjana Hariprasad, Radhika Vora, Rajesh Bhatia, Mallika Swaminadhan and B. S. Bhatnagar were the ideal combination of people who read various versions of the drafts and gave incisive inputs. This group was perfect because they covered all generations from Gen Z to baby boomers.

Finally, to my family:

Siddharth, here is your 'fourth key'—the message you wanted for your children. Your persistence left me with no choice but to just do it.

Meghna, your calm, methodical and professional background taught me that talking to hundreds of people and writing articles is a lot different from trying to put your thoughts in a book. You helped me think the process through.

Rahul and Rohini, the fact that you have featured prominently in my stories tells you how much you have taught me. As usual, I would always like the last word with you, so I am happy to believe that I have taught you well for you to teach me in turn!

Finally, my biggest fan and supporter, Thangam. Forty-four years ago, I would never have imagined that marriage was a three-in-one deal for me. Thanks to you I have got happiness, success and meaning in these years. *Yeh dil* could not have asked for more. A big thanks cannot say it all.

ABOUT THE AUTHOR

Photo: Darshan H.N.

Ramesh Venkateswaran has donned many hats over the years. After a successful stint in the corporate world and as a corporate consultant and trainer, he has devoted his time to teaching. He is an adjunct faculty member at his alma mater, the Indian Institute of Management, Bangalore, for close to three decades. He has also headed The Lawrence School Lovedale, Nilgiris, and SDM Institute for Management Development, Mysuru.

Ramesh is a co-founder, chairman and volunteer at Vishwas, Society for Mental Health, Bengaluru, a not-for-profit organization that offers free counselling to people in emotional stress.

He can be reached at rameshvenkat20@gmail.com.